“Purity rings. Abstinenc[illegible] bringing awesome married sex. These—and many other practices and teachings—have characterized evangelical purity culture. And they’ve done some damage. In *Talking Back to Purity Culture*, Rachel Joy Welcher holds to a high view of Scripture and its sexual ethic, challenges prosperity thinking, and calls Christians to a better way—one that celebrates embodied living at any age or stage, views others as creatures worthy of respect, and has as its focus the glory of God. I can’t think of one demographic that wouldn’t benefit from this book.”

Sandra Glahn, professor at Dallas Theological Seminary and coauthor of *Sanctified Sexuality*

“*Talking Back to Purity Culture* is saturated with gospel truth and clarity that confronts the overwhelmingly legalistic, shaming, and hopeless rubric of purity culture—especially the ways in which it blames young women for the sins of their brothers and fathers. Parents, and especially you moms, it’s time to speak the truth to your children about sexuality and to assure your daughters of their worth as created in God’s image. I’m thrilled to recommend this wonderful book.”

Elyse Fitzpatrick, author of *Worthy: Celebrating the Value of Women*

“Impeccably researched, gently written, and a timely word for those who grew up kissing dating goodbye, wearing purity rings, attending abstinence rallies, and waiting (perhaps waiting still) for their ‘one.’ Welcher is deft in her exploration of what went right and what went wrong for the lives of millions of Christians—before marriage *and* after it—and she is careful in her admonition to future leaders and lovers. A needed and healing work.”

Lore Ferguson Wilbert, author of *Handle With Care: How Jesus Redeems the Power of Touch in Life and Ministry*

“Rachel Joy Welcher’s book is a God-honoring and human-dignifying work that will help people find healing for sins, for shame, and from abuses inflicted on them. It is one I wish I’d had available during my teen years and twenties as I navigated purity culture and came out pretty lost. Rachel offers such a pointed, gracious corrective to the many missteps and also a clear, hopeful, honoring path forward for women and men alike whose perspective on sexuality and purity has been skewed by this culture. I’m so grateful for her strong, gracious words helping readers understand what purity means to God, not just as a fabricated culture.”

Barnabas Piper, author and podcaster

"Rachel Welcher writes with biblical clarity and Jesus-centering grace as she probes the smoldering ashes of purity culture. For those who grew up under its teaching, for those who propagated it in good faith, and even for strangers to it like me, she offers a gift: not just a critique, but a vision for something better. She gently shows that taking God at his Word—not adding to it or subtracting from it—is that better way and invites us to walk in it."

Rachel Gilson, author of *Born Again This Way: Coming Out, Coming to Faith, and What Comes Next*

"This book is a must-read for anyone who is looking for a thoughtful and thoroughly researched reconsideration of purity culture teachings. Rachel has done a masterful job of synthesizing decades of Christian literature on the subject into a sincere biblical critique of purity culture. But most importantly, Rachel casts a vision for the reader to move forward with compassionate yet faithful teaching on the subject, and she gives practical application for parents, leaders, teens, and singles alike."

Jessica Van Der Wyngaard, director of *I Survived I Kissed Dating Goodbye* and cohost of the *Where Do We Go from Here?* podcast

"As an educator of college students for more than three decades, I understand well the difficulties in helping young people sort through the mixed messages from both the church and the culture regarding sex. It is easy, in correcting the falsehoods of the world, to make errors in the opposite direction. Rachel Joy Welcher navigates these tensions scripturally, wisely, and compassionately—and does so within a wide range of topics of concern to people of all ages and all stages of life. *Talking Back to Purity Culture* is a book I will recommend over and over, not only to my students but to all who are striving toward a more holistic and biblical understanding of human sexuality in these times."

Karen Swallow Prior, author of *On Reading Well* and *Fierce Convictions*

"I typically bristle at the mention of purity culture because I often think it's an excuse for the church to reject a good and flourishing sexual ethic and the importance of training our children. And yet I find myself reading Rachel Welcher's work with interest because she is saying some very important things for Christians to heed. Rachel calls us to reject both a works-based futility and a hedonistic lifestyle; both lead to spiritual poverty. Instead, Rachel urges us to adopt a gospel-centered sexual ethic that is countercultural in both its approach and in its pathways to grace. So read this book and learn from one of the most gifted writers of our time, and be drawn, once again, to the beautiful and sacred old paths God has laid out for us."

Daniel Darling, pastor and author of *The Characters of Christmas* and *The Dignity Revolution*

TALKING BACK TO PURITY CULTURE

REDISCOVERING FAITHFUL CHRISTIAN SEXUALITY

RACHEL JOY WELCHER

FOREWORD BY SCOTT SAULS

IVP
An imprint of InterVarsity Press
Downers Grove, Illinois

InterVarsity Press
P.O. Box 1400, Downers Grove, IL 60515-1426
ivpress.com
email@ivpress.com

InterVarsity Press® is the book-publishing division of InterVarsity Christian Fellowship/USA®, a movement of students and faculty active on campus at hundreds of universities, colleges, and schools of nursing in the United States of America, and a member movement of the International Fellowship of Evangelical Students. For information about local and regional activities, visit intervarsity.org.

Cover design and image composite: David Fassett
Interior design: Daniel van Loon
Images: white photoframes montage: © AlexeyVS / iStock / Getty Images Plus

ISBN 978-0-8308-4816-4 (print)
ISBN 978-0-8308-4817-1 (digital)

Printed in the United States of America ♾

InterVarsity Press is committed to ecological stewardship and to the conservation of natural resources in all our operations. This book was printed using sustainably sourced paper.

Library of Congress Cataloging-in-Publication Data
A catalog record for this book is available from the Library of Congress.

P 25 24 23 22 21 20 19 18 17 16 15 14 13 12 11 10 9 8 7 6 5 4 3 2 1
Y 37 36 35 34 33 32 31 30 29 28 27 26 25 24 23 22 21 20

To the hurting, the abused, and the angry; the weary, the curious, and the skeptical. To those whose faith is smaller than a mustard seed, and to those who, after experiencing the rough and tumble of life, still cling to the hem of Jesus' robe: you will not be put to shame.

CONTENTS

FOREWORD

Scott Sauls

It has been said that in and following the New Testament era, Christians were widely known for being promiscuous with their money and conservative with their bodies.

Their so-called financial promiscuity was directed toward the work of God and the needs of the poor, while their bodily "conservatism" reflected their belief in a vision for sex and marriage passed on to them by Moses, the prophets and apostles, and Jesus himself. This vision affirms the sometimes-scandalous belief that sexual intercourse—a glorious gift from God given chiefly for human intimacy, pleasure, and procreation—is reserved uniquely for marriage between one man and one woman.

According to many in our late modern times, such a limiting view of sex and marriage seems preposterous. According to one Harvard student in her impassioned defense of college hookup culture, "For me, being a strong woman means not being ashamed that I like to have sex. . . . To say that I have to care about every person I have sex with is an unreasonable expectation. It feels good! It feels good!"[1]

It may come as a surprise to some that ancient cultures were just as appalled by "Christian sexuality" as their twenty-first-century counterparts are. The sexual revolution is no recent phenomenon but is as old as time itself.

Then as now, in most instances, the men fared better than the women.

From the earliest pages of Scripture, even highly esteemed patriarchs would pleasure themselves with prostitutes, accumulate multiple wives and concubines, and "spill their seed" on the ground in an act of loveless passion. Abraham, the father of all who have faith, offered his wife up to sexual predators in an effort to save his own skin. King David abused his power when he "saw" and then "took" Bathsheba, his next-door neighbor and wife of one of his closest, most loyal friends. Lacking in all subtlety, the disciple Matthew records that "David was the father of Solomon, whose mother had been Uriah's wife" (Matthew 1:6). In New Testament Corinth, a man in the church had sexual relations with his stepmother. And adultery was defined by Jesus as not only the physical act but also lustful fantasy.

That's just a sampling from among those who *did* believe in God. And then there were the Romans, a brutish and godless power culture that also lived by the double standard. It was the rule, not the exception, for prominent men of Rome to be sexually involved with multiple mistresses as well as a younger man or two in addition to their wives. Women, on the other hand, were not allowed such "freedoms." Likewise, if a woman gave birth to a girl, the husband would decide whether they should keep the child or throw her away—akin to a post-partum abortion as it were.

In our twenty-first-century context, we would like to think of ourselves as more enlightened, as if we have somehow progressed beyond such ugly human realities. But have we? The emergence of and growing popularity of pornography, nonmarried cohabitation, LGBTQ+ concerns and culture, polyamorous arrangements, and hookup culture attest otherwise.

What's more, the #MeToo movement has arisen and emboldened women and their allies to (finally) say, "No more!" to predatory and perverted men. Many well-known celebrities and influencers have lent their names and platforms to advance the #MeToo cause. At the same time, many of these same celebrities and influencers have also, on those very same platforms, lauded and eulogized the late Hugh Hefner, the famed sex mogul who championed a climate in which the use, abuse, objectification, and subjugation of women could flourish as a civil rights hero.

As it was in ancient times, so it is today. Ours is a culture of sexual confusion, oppression, and slavery that masks itself as a culture of sexual freedom.

In reaction to a hypersexualized world, the Christian purity culture was born. While well-intended in some respects, the purity movement would, not unlike its sexual revolution counterpart, overswing the pendulum and become its own version of a culture of shame. Not only would unmarried people be told to avoid sex but also all forms of kissing, holding hands, and dating. Men and boys were rightly encouraged to do battle against lust and flee from sexual immorality. To help the men succeed, women and girls were *wrongly* blamed for "making" men stumble by dressing immodestly (whatever that means). Likewise, married women were admonished for "not putting out enough" in the marriage beds, thus causing their (often emotionally unavailable) husbands' eyes to wander.

In the sexual revolution climate, what is needed is not less sexual freedom but better and healthier sexual freedom. Those who are unmarried (like the apostle Paul and Jesus Christ) are free to embrace countercultural chastity as a high, holy, and praiseworthy calling. In doing so, these men and women affirm God's unique design for sex and in so doing protect their own souls from injury. Sex works a lot like fire. When removed from its protective boundaries, it burns us and leaves scars. When brought and kept inside those covenanted boundaries, a sweet foretaste of the ultimate love feast between Christ and his Bride, the Church, is given.

But the picture God paints of healthy, life-giving sexuality is also different than the one from the old TV show *Leave It to Beaver* in which Ward and June shared a bedroom but slept in separate beds. Instead, the Maker of sex and marriage tells husbands to "rejoice in the wife of your youth" and "may her breasts satisfy you always, may you ever be intoxicated with her love" (Proverbs 5:18-19). He tells Adam and Eve, the first married couple, to fully consummate their naked-and-without-shame state by coming together as one flesh (Genesis 2:24). He brings us into the bedroom of the "she" and the "he" of the Song of Songs, where husband and wife recite erotic poetry and sing erotic love songs over one another's naked bodies. Centuries later, Paul, the unmarried apostle, commands able-bodied husbands and wives to enjoy sexual intercourse often, except in temporary Lenten-like seasons of prayer and fasting because his body belongs to her and her body belongs to him (1 Corinthians 7:4).

Likewise, God paints a picture of compassion, grace, and empathy toward those who have been burned, even reduced to ashes, through the mishandling of sex. A mob of men prepares to execute a woman caught in the act of adultery, but Jesus steps in and shows mercy to her. Maybe Jesus steps in because of the injustice of it all, since the mob of men are making her bear the penalty of a two-party transgression all by herself. As was customary, the adulterous man escaped accountability, leaving the woman alone to bear all of the shame. Sound familiar? Or maybe Jesus steps in because the woman's sin evokes in him more compassion than judgment, more grace than condemnation, and more mercy than justice (John 8:1-11). For as Charles Spurgeon once said, God loves to forgive our sin even more than we love to commit it.

There is also the Canaanite prostitute Rahab, who is sovereignly and lovingly placed in the ancestry of Jesus alongside Tamar, a destitute and abandoned widow who posed as a prostitute (Matthew 1:3, 5). And of course, there was the other prostitute who barged into a dinner party uninvited and wiped Jesus' feet with her hair and her tears and anointed him with her perfume and her lips—the primary tools of her trade—to demonstrate her affection in the only way she knew how. Jesus was not disgusted by her, he was not ashamed to be called her elder brother. No, he instead delighted in her and declared that she who loved much had also been forgiven much (Luke 7:36-50).

What is needed in our late modern times . . . what is needed not only in our own culture but in every culture as well as every bedroom, every boardroom, every big screen, every TV screen, and every computer screen, is a well-articulated, biblically grounded, compelling, and life-giving answer to the shame of promiscuity culture on the one hand and the shame of purity culture on the other. What's needed is a freshly painted yet anciently grounded vision for sex, marriage, singleness, gender, and love that upholds and advances conviction *and* compassion. I believe that Rachel has done a masterful job painting that vision for us in this book. I trust that you will also.

INTRODUCTION

It's Time to Talk Back

I was in high school when Joshua Harris's book *I Kissed Dating Goodbye* captured the attention of the evangelical world. It kicked off a movement and inspired countless other books on dating and sexual purity. I read many of these, internalizing messages about my responsibility as a female to keep men from lusting, the value of my virginity, and how sexual sin could destroy my future marriage. I often finished these books more ashamed of my sexuality than when I had started them. Marriage and sex were placed on a pedestal, and they quickly became an idol: something I thought would one day complete me.

With my first serious relationship, I tried to follow all I'd been told in the books. We were friends first. We dated for years before getting engaged and were engaged for six months before getting married. My father officiated the ceremony. My best friend made the cake. I even saved my first kiss for him. But before our fifth wedding anniversary, he had a crisis of faith and walked away from God and our marriage. The books I had read promised that premarital purity would result in a flourishing marriage. They told me that sexual obedience would secure a specific blessing. When the reward didn't come, I was left to wonder what I had done wrong and whether others who had grown up reading the same books and hearing the same messages were wrestling with similar questions.

I taught English in private Christian high schools for a decade. Studying literature with teenagers creates a depth of conversation that small talk never could. As a class, we would reflect on the joys and struggles different characters faced, and this naturally led my students to open up about their own stories: what they feared, what was going on at home, and their hopes for the future. This dialogue also created space for students to share about sexuality. Over the years, I have talked with students who were sexually abused, addicted to pornography, wrestling with same-sex attraction, worried about sex, excited about sex, sexually abstinent, and sexually active. What I noticed was how many were living in shame, afraid to talk about their God-given sexuality in anything above a whisper.

The classroom isn't the only place I heard these confessions. I grew up in a pastor's home, and I watched my parents love the vulnerable. There were often people in our living room or at the kitchen table who were heavy with the trials of life. My parents would feed them, listen to them, and pray over them. And as I grew into adulthood in the church, I began a similar ministry to the hurting. People sought me out for prayer, counsel, and friendship. Their stories in relation to sexuality were just as complicated as my students'—filled with guilt, abuse, fear, and hope. And when my peers and I were honest with one another, we shared similar stories.

So when it came time to pick a dissertation topic for my master's thesis in divinity at the University of St. Andrews, I thought about these questions and struggles. I wondered how teachings that I had internalized, such as the idea that women are responsible for the purity of men or that you can earn a perfect marriage by practicing chastity, held up next to Scripture, and I decided to wade back into the purity teachings of my youth to find out.

This book isn't a new *I Kissed Dating Goodbye*, nor is it meant to be the ultimate source or guide for sexual purity. My hope is that it will push Christians to engage with these topics together, in community. This book is for anyone trying to sort out what sexual purity means and how to talk about it—youth leaders, pastors, parents, teenagers, and those who grew up in church during the high tide of purity culture. It is for those who want to reevaluate what they were previously taught (or have taught others). It is for the hopeful and the bitter; those who underlined every other line in *I Kissed Dating Goodbye* and those who burned the book in college. It is for Christians who want to honor God and want to see the church do better.

As I wrote this book, I found myself filled with a righteous anger at a Christian subculture that, for years, has made false promises and worshiped the idol of chastity rather than the Lord Jesus Christ. We have so much to uproot. We have so much to talk about. But I need you to know something before I go any further: I love the church. If I critique her, it is as a member of the body of Christ and a fellow sinner-saint. I pray for her flourishing. My desire to reevaluate purity culture teachings is out of love for the church, not a vendetta against her.

I will not be proposing a new sexual ethic for Christians or calling into question the validity of Scripture. God is above critique. But we are not. And I believe that humility demands regular reflection on our spiritual practices and biblical interpretation. This is not "wishy-washy" but rather a recognition of our proneness to wander, an acknowledgment that we all have a human weakness and fallibility and that everyone is susceptible to getting so caught up in something that we forget to tether ourselves to God's Word.

Evangelical purity culture was not a wicked movement but rather an earnest response to the age-old problem of immorality and the modern crisis of STDs and teenage pregnancy.

As with most earnest, human responses, we didn't get everything right. Surprised? I'm not. I won't get everything right in this book either. But it's time to step back and look at the movement that shaped so many of us—our relationships, our self-image, and our Christian faith. It's time to talk back to purity culture.[1]

1

FROM RINGS AND PLEDGES TO CONVERSATION IN COMMUNITY

I recently spoke at a conference on sexuality at a church in North Tulsa. At every plenary session, workshop, and panel, I heard people address topics out loud that most of us deal with in private. A young woman shared about the years she spent being sex-trafficked by her own father, and how Jesus transformed her life and gave her hope. There was a panel discussion about same-sex attraction, one about singleness, and another about how the church responds to sexual assault. Words like *masturbation* were spoken aloud instead of being merely hinted at, and in all of this there was no intent to titillate or create shock value or cause nervous laughter. The mood was one of contrition and compassion.

Alongside conviction, I felt years of sexual shame sliding off my shoulders. As I looked around, I saw tear-streaked faces. A hush bathed the room not because of guilt but because dark things were coming to light. Burdens, lies, questions, and struggles were being brought from the chill of isolation into the warmth of community. I have never experienced anything quite like it.

MODERN EVANGELICAL PURITY CULTURE

The Christian community I was raised in, in late twentieth and early twenty-first century America, tried to tame teenage sexuality by promoting an "evangelical Christian purity culture"—a movement that utilized pledges, books, and events to promote sexual abstinence outside of marriage.[1] Although the idea of a purity culture certainly exists in other places besides America, and in other religious contexts, Christine Gardner, author of *Making Chastity Sexy,* sees American evangelical Christians "at the center of the promotion of sexual abstinence."[2]

In her book *The Scarlett Virgins: When Sex Replaces Salvation,* Rebecca Lemke points out that purity culture "allowed many [parents] to skirt the responsibility of discussing sex with their child while simultaneously believing that the issue was being addressed through 'role models' and purity events"—and, I would add, through *books.*[3] Our choice to detach the topic of sexual purity from regular conversation has isolated it from the whole of Scripture and life, turning questions that are meant to press us further into prayer, the church, and God's Word, into books, conferences, and websites. But the subject of sexual purity is too nuanced to squeeze into one book or conference. It must be integrated into our regular conversations.

THE BOOKS THAT MADE US

Too many of us are weighed down by sexual expectations, pressures, and shame. I interviewed a woman who lost her husband to cancer when their first child was just two years old and she was pregnant with their second. She told me that she has spent more time in counseling working through damaging purity culture teachings than she has dealing with the pain of widowhood. How is that possible?

The answer is nuanced. There were conferences. Camps. Youth group messages. True Love Waits rallies. Stories and songs. Purity rings. But for many of us, we need look no further than the teetering stack of purity-themed books on our childhood nightstand. Books. We read about it in books.

One year, I put a quote by Francis Bacon on my classroom wall that said: "Some books are to be tasted, others to be swallowed, and some few to be chewed and digested." Books that were meant to be tasted began filling the shelves in Christian bookstores, and parents bought them for their teenagers, who swallowed them whole. There was an assumption that anything about purity written by a Christian would be not only safe but helpful.

But we didn't read these books the way we were forced to read *Hamlet* or *The Grapes of Wrath* in English class, laboring over themes and analyzing worldviews. Instead, we picked up *Wild at Heart* and *I Kissed Dating Goodbye*, never bothering to chew a word before we made it part of ourselves. We read *Every Man's Battle* and *For Young Women Only* by ourselves, interpreting and internalizing messages in isolation from community, without any discussion or debate. We carried them like Bibles.

During my graduate research, I studied those popular Christian books on gender and purity written in the late 1990s and early 2000s—books like *I Kissed Dating Goodbye, And the Bride Wore White, Every Man's Battle, Romance God's Way,* and *Wild at Heart.* Some of you are familiar with these books. Maybe you wore a "purity ring" or remember hearing Rebecca St. James sing "Wait for Me" on the radio. Maybe there's a True Love Waits pledge card tucked into your Bible from junior high. Or maybe you didn't grow up in the church during this time and your exposure to purity culture has come from little snippets you've heard from other Christians or those who have left the church, complaining or rejoicing about how the movement affected them.

I posed this question to my Twitter followers not too long ago: What do you think of when you hear the term "purity culture"? Here are some of the responses I got.

> If I follow a certain set of rules, most of which aren't even Biblical, I'm guaranteed a wonderful marriage with a great sex life.[4]
>
> His lust is your fault.[5]
>
> The well-meaning desire for protection with a list of what-to-do's buried among deficient whys.[6]
>
> A culture of fear that doesn't tell the truth about sex or the character of God.[7]
>
> Preemptive punishment that follows from placing unfair and inappropriate responsibility on others.[8]
>
> Fear and shame. It brought men's struggles with lust to the forefront but offered no hope for women with similar struggles.[9]

It is safe to say that modern American evangelical purity culture is a trigger topic for many, and critique of the movement is gaining momentum. Pastor Nadia Bolz-Weber, author of *Shameless: A Sexual Reformation*, recently tweeted a call for women to send her their old purity rings so she could have them melted down and made into a "sculpture of a vagina."[10]

Even former leaders of the movement, such as *I Kissed Dating Goodbye* author Josh Harris, are reevaluating the messages they made popular. Harris recently wrote a public statement saying: "While I stand by my book's call to sincerely love others, my thinking has changed significantly in the past twenty years." He went on to admit that he now thinks "dating can be a healthy part of a person developing relationally" and that his book "emphasized practices (not dating, not kissing before marriage) and concepts (giving your heart away) that are not in the Bible."[11]

Harris's book defined an era. What changed his mind? Listening to others. He began hearing stories from people who had been hurt by his book, and instead of ignoring the criticism, he leaned into it. In Jessica Van Der Wyngaard's documentary *I Survived I Kissed Dating Goodbye,* Harris says: "You can change your mind about things." And while Harris went on to change his mind about more than just purity culture—recently announcing his divorce from his wife and his departure from the Christian faith—I believe that re-evaluation has value for the Christian.[12] It's part of being human, and it's necessary for our growth, which is what this book is about: leaning into tough questions together.

RETHINKING PURITY CULTURE

At the end of my seminar on purity culture myths at that conference in Tulsa, a father raised his hand and asked: "What books *can* you recommend?" He had a teenage daughter. And his question made sense. I had spent the majority of my lecture quoting from popular purity books, pointing out their damaging messages about sex, marriage, and gender. If not those books, which ones *could* he hand his daughter? Which were safe? I paused. And at that moment I realized the answer to sexual purity will never be found in a book slid under a teenager's door.

So I told him: "There are good things in many of these books." And I meant it. "But," I said, "I can't think of a single one that I would recommend reading in isolation. What we need more of is conversation. Instead of trying to find the perfect book, let's keep talking about sexuality and purity out loud. Together. In community. Pick up any of these books, but read them with someone else and, whatever you do, keep the dialogue going."

In the following chapters, I will ask you to join me in reevaluating certain purity culture messages such as the idolization of virginity; marriage and sex as the reward for chastity; men as lust machines, and women as responsible for the purity of men. And I will ask you to consider ways we can move forward from these teachings as a church, specifically regarding how we talk about sex and sexuality; overcome unbiblical stereotypes about men and women; address the neglected realities of female sexuality, same-sex attraction, perpetual singleness, painful sex, and infertility; define sexual abuse and treat its victims; respond to sexual sin; talk to our children about their bodies, friendships, dating, masturbation, pornography, and so on; and move forward from hurtful purity culture messages into truth, grace, and community.

In the first few chapters, I lay a foundation of what purity culture taught us about these questions. Rather than merely *telling* you, I want to *show* you by drawing from some of the most popular Christian books of the late 1990s and early 2000s. This will involve some active reading and, I hope, plenty of conversation. I will add my own commentary and pushback as the chapters build, and I will eventually lay out for you what I believe to be a biblical sexual ethic and some practical ways we can faithfully and graciously live it out as a church.

I cannot stress enough the importance of taking any thoughts, confessions, or hurt that this book brings out into the light of community and God's grace. If you are reading alone right now, please make it a goal to bring at least one of these topics into real-life conversation with someone else. I can't promise it will always be comfortable, but we have to start somewhere. In writing this book, I have forced myself to have these conversations. In fact, I have interviewed over one hundred people at this point—formally and informally—asking about their experiences with purity teachings and how they feel about those messages now. I talked with some people over coffee and others via email or video chat. Just last month, I talked to three young women for an hour in the kitchen during a baby shower. People *want* to talk about this subject, but it's difficult to start the conversation.

DISCUSSION QUESTIONS

1. What were you taught about sex and marriage growing up?
2. What comes to your mind when you hear the term "purity culture"?
3. What connection (if any) do you have with the purity movement? How did it affect you?
4. Which teachings from purity culture do you appreciate and/or believe are biblical?
5. Which teachings from purity culture do you find troubling? Why?
6. What do you think of the ways people are critiquing/criticizing purity culture today?
7. What keeps us from having an open, honest dialogue about sexual purity?

ACTIVITY

One way to start this conversation is to get a group together to watch Jessica Van Der Wyngaard's documentary starring Joshua Harris called *I Survived I Kissed Dating Goodbye.*[13] It's a good introduction to the topic of purity culture for those who didn't grow up in it, but it also holds meaning for those who did. The more diverse your group, the better. For example, if everyone is married, you'll miss out on the valuable perspective of singles and how purity culture has affected them and the way they view their singleness. Likewise, if your group is only made up of singles, you'll miss out on the perspective of those who are married, and how purity culture messages line up with the reality of marriage. Invite widows and teenagers. Consider opening up your home for a viewing party and a discussion afterward.

2

THE IDOLIZATION OF VIRGINITY

Amy Deneson was given her first purity ring when she was thirteen years old. "Accepting it meant I promised to stay a virgin until my wedding night—to keep my mind innocent, my body untouched, my soul blameless—so that I could one day present my husband with the ultimate gift," she said.[1] Deneson viewed her ring as a visible sign of her countercultural commitment to remain a virgin until marriage. When the heart-shaped stone fell out of the ring one day during basketball practice, she panicked, concerned that a damaged purity ring might foreshadow some threat to her sexual purity.

VIRGINITY AS WORTH

If purity culture were a throne, virginity would be the queen sitting on it. It's presented not only as a God-honoring pursuit but as a determinant of personal value. Roses are passed around rooms full of nervous teenagers, then held up, crumpled and bruised, with fewer petals, as an example of what happens to those who give their virginity away. Paper is ripped in half. "The pastor explained that we could never get our purity back—it was like water that had been spit in or gum that had been chewed," Rebecca Lemke writes.[2] This idea was especially emphasized to women. Sara Moslener, purity culture historian and author of *Virgin Nation: Sexual Purity and American Adolescence*, notes how James Dobson painted a picture of "female sexuality as a commodity that reach[es] the height of its value on the wedding day."[3] A woman's worth rests not in her soul but between her legs, as if virginity were some remnant of pre-fall righteousness, untainted by Adam and Eve's sin, which a woman can protect if she is hypervigilant enough.

When virginity is painted this way, as the greatest gift one can give their spouse, those who lose their virginity before marriage are seen as having less to offer. Their only choice is to try to gather the fallen petals of their personal worth into the shape of a bouquet as best they can. The concept of "second" or "renewed" virginity is a common theme in purity rhetoric, but the trauma of these visual metaphors speaks louder than any footnote about second chances. One might be able to seek forgiveness and recommit to chastity but "it's difficult to repair a broken china cup."[4]

I love what Debra Hirsch says in her book *Redeeming Sex*: "Every human being on the planet is sexually broken . . . all of us are on a journey toward wholeness; not one of us is excluded."[5] Whether someone is a virgin, has been raped, or has "slept around," we are all broken from the fall. We all need Jesus. And thankfully our value as image bearers is not dependent on our sexual past. In his recent book *The Dignity Revolution*, Daniel Darling writes: "You were valuable before you did anything."[6] And I would add, you are just as valuable, even if you have done many things that fall short of the righteousness of God. Jesus has taken those failings and abuses on himself, crucifying them on the cross.

VIRGINITY AS PURITY

I am thankful that in this sex-saturated world my parents told me where sex belongs—in marriage—and my church reaffirmed it. I am glad that I had sex for the first time on my wedding night. If I ever have children, I will teach them what the Bible says about sex, that it was created by God to be an act of unifying self-giving within the marriage covenant between one man and one woman. I will teach them that, in marriage, sex is a God-honoring good, but that extramarital sex is a sin against a holy and loving Father. But I will not tell them that virginity makes them pure.

I may have been a virgin when I got married, but I was already a sexual sinner. As a young believer, my virgin status kept me from recognizing this. It was so easy to justify my lust and selfishness by telling myself: "You have never even kissed a boy." I knew plenty of others who had not only kissed their boyfriends but had done a lot more. My childhood best friend was pregnant by the age of fifteen. Surely I was sexually pure by comparison.

But I was not. Jesus' words from the Sermon on the Mount are chilling in their inclusivity: anyone who looks at another person with lust has committed adultery with them in their heart. I may have been a virgin when I got married, but I was also an adulterer. Virginity means only that an individual has never decided to or been forced to have sexual intercourse with another person. It is not a badge of holiness, a sign of sexual purity, or a ticket to heaven.

The term "technical virginity" exists because of how inventive we are when it comes to finding sexual activities outside of sexual intercourse. While I have known Christians who refuse to even hold hands before marriage, others, pointing to virginity as the definition of sexual purity, are willing to engage in anything from mutual masturbation to oral sex, avoiding *only* the act of genital penetration. Virginity as purity neglects Jesus' call for the pursuit of whole-person purity, which includes not only the hymen but our whole body, mind, and heart.

To understand purity culture's emphasis on virginity, we must recognize that the Bible has not been the only influence behind the movement. Much of modern purity culture has been shaped by our nationwide reaction to the threat of STDs and teenage pregnancy, brought on by the sexual revolution of the 1960s to the 1980s. Linda Kay Klein, author of *Pure: Inside the Evangelical Movement That Shamed a Generation of Young Women and How I Broke Free*, points out: "Americans were scared. AIDS was killing people by the thousands, there were growing concerns about other sexually transmitted infections. . . . And many conservatives believed the return to traditional values, including chastity, was the only solution."[7]

One of the greatest tensions in the modern Christian purity movement has been federally funded abstinence education. Groups like Silver Ring Thing (founded by Christians) recognized that their message could go much further if they accepted government help. While Silver Ring Thing accepted the funds, founder Denny Pattyn was "disgusted by the government's insistence that his abstinence work be devoid of all religious content," believing that true change takes place in individuals through the power of the Holy Spirit.[8] Still, federal funding meant that more teenagers would be exposed to abstinence as an option.

Abstinence education has been supported with federal funds under the last four presidents, and according to *The Hill*, abstinence-only education is "making a comeback" under current president Donald Trump.[9] One question Christians need to ask is: What happens to the message of sexual purity when it is taught apart from Christ? Whether one is for or against government-funded abstinence education, it is a question worth pondering.

VIRGINITY AS IDENTITY

Appealing to modern American teenagers meant emphasizing rebellion and identity. Strategies for attracting teenagers to chastity had to focus more on individual benefits and consequences than the glory of God. Christine Gardner says that the abstinence events she attended were full of live concerts and personal testimonials.[10] The books I read growing up focused on how my sexual behavior would impact *my* life, *my* reputation, and *my* marriage.

The American shift toward individualism, with our "army of one" commercials and our idolization of the "personal journey," seeped into evangelical culture. Growing up, the emphasis was on "me and Jesus" more than my role as a member of the body of Christ. I didn't even become familiar with the term "common good" in regard to Christian theology until I began graduate school in my early thirties.

Modern purity teachings harnessed individualism, depicting sexual self-restraint as a choice for "self-care" and a way to ensure a future satisfying sex life within marriage.[11] And for a time, abstinence was trending. I remember celebrities such as Britney Spears and Jessica Simpson wearing purity rings. Later, young stars such as the Jonas Brothers and Miley Cyrus kept the trend going. Gardner notes that purity rhetoric essentially borrows the feminist message of "my body, my choice" in order to convince teenagers that sexual abstinence is about asserting their agency.[12] The purity movement tried to make chastity attractive by highlighting the rebellion required to say no to premarital sex in a culture so used to saying yes.

The emphasis on personal choice included a public element. This is where purity rings, necklaces, and events like father/daughter purity balls came into vogue. One woman I interviewed said her dad brought home a ring from Italy for her to wear, to symbolize her commitment to chastity. The purity ring given by one's parents or purchased at abstinence events such as Silver Ring Thing even became a part of some wedding ceremonies.

Another woman, Nicole, told me that she viewed her virginity as "a badge of honor." She wore a purity ring until the day she got married and on her wedding day, "my dad took the ring off, then handed it to my groom." "I cringe to think of that now," she added.

"What about that memory makes you cringe?" I asked. She responded:

> My motivations were off. My husband and I met in high school and dated for several years before we got married. I think part of me wanted to protect my reputation. See, everybody? We really did wait. I also think so much of my identity at the time was wrapped up in being the good Christian girl. The whole ceremony reminds me of the Pharisees. I feel like I was saying, "Look at me—I'm so pure, I'm so holy," when my heart was full of pride and fear.
>
> Also, I no longer see purity as a gift one spouse gives to another. God has made me pure through Christ, and he alone keeps me pure. Purity, then, is mainly about me and God, not me and my husband. Sexual purity is the natural overflow of humbly placing myself under God's authority, acknowledging my own sinfulness, and depending on Christ to help me walk in holiness. When I am living in purity, my husband and my marriage definitely benefit. But that is God's grace, not my own doing.

Nicole describes exactly what can go wrong when sexual purity is motivated by personal identity and the approval of others more than the glory of God. While she made it to the altar a virgin, her story still holds regret due to wrong motivations for right actions.

Another woman, Stephanie, told me: "I went to the purity class, I had the ring, but inside I was torn apart by my hidden sin." While highlighting individualism might be a brilliant rhetorical tactic, these motivators eventually crumble when they come up against other equally self-centered desires. Pursuing sexual purity for the sake of one's identity and reputation is a foundation built on shifting sand.

Virginity-as-identity has caused some to experience unnecessary guilt and confusion when they finally experience sex in marriage. If you've listened to people talk about growing up in purity culture for any length of time, you've probably heard the "light switch" analogy—the expectation that one can transition from being completely virginal to sexually uninhibited on their honeymoon, as quickly as flipping a light switch. But many Christians have struggled to find the light switch, especially those who saw virginity as part of their identity.

The writers of *Jane the Virgin,* a television dramedy series, captured this tension in the episode where Jane, the main character, finally loses her virginity. Having grown up Catholic, she chose to wait to have sex until marriage. When she and her husband finally consummate their union, instead of feeling joy, Jane feels disconnected from herself. She wonders who she is now that she is not a virgin.[13]

For some people, sex within marriage, which is meant to unite a couple and bring them joy and pleasure, is accompanied by shame. This is especially common for Christian women. I talked to a young bride recently who confessed that, growing up in the church, the only thing she heard about sex was "don't do it." Now, two years into marriage and after the birth of their first child, she told me: "I still struggle with feeling dirty, slutty, and sinful when I'm intimate with my husband."

Because female sexuality is often downplayed in purity culture, there's an extra layer of guilt for Christian women, not only about committing sexual sin but about their identity as sexual beings. This shame can lead women to demonize their God-given sexuality and can also, in turn, make the "switch" from virgin to sexually active in marriage a time of guilt rather than joy. Linda Kay Klein notes how confusing this message can be for women:

> The purity movement teaches us that a "pure" woman comes to her husband an untouched virgin who has hardly (if ever) thought about sex before. And then, naturally and beautifully, the woman's new husband introduces his wife to sexuality for the first time and years of pent-up sexual energy which she was not even aware of come pouring out of her, allowing her to meet her new husband's every sexual want, which is also her every want, and together they live happily ever after. Both the repressed sexuality of the virgin and the fully surrendered sexuality of the wife are requirements of purity culture—one being fabled to lead to the other.[14]

Returning to the example from *Jane the Virgin*, it is interesting that Jane feels the pressure to fake an orgasm during her first experience with sex. When her husband finds out that she lied, he is confused, but the viewer sees the situation very clearly: sex has been built up in Jane's mind for years, and she wants her first experience to be perfect, especially for her husband. Jane's fictional experience illustrates a truth I heard repeatedly from those I interviewed: the transition from virgin to sexually active in marriage is nothing like turning on a light switch.

SEXUAL SELF-CONTROL IS A LIFELONG PURSUIT

Purity culture's obsession with virginity also obscures the fact that our call to sexual purity is lifelong. Adolescents are encouraged that if they just hold out for a little while they will soon get married and be able to unleash all their sexual energy on another person. Not only does this dehumanize image bearers of God by painting them as nothing more than sexual outlets, it depicts the pursuit of purity as a season in life rather than a lifelong calling. Books and resources about sexual purity focus mainly on young singles rather than addressing Christians in all circumstances.

A friend of mine, Laura, shared an interesting story that highlights our need for a lifelong commitment to purity—and it also gave me a new appreciation for purity rings. She said that she was given her ring at age fourteen and she wore it up until the day she got married. On her wedding night, she gave it to her husband. "It was beautiful, and I was so thankful that I'd waited," Laura said. But a few months later, she was horrified to discover that she felt attracted to someone else: "I guess I'd naively thought that marriage (and great sex) would resolve the whole purity problem." She decided to find her purity ring, which was nestled in her husband's sock drawer, and put it back on her finger again, as a reminder to herself and to her husband that she was still committed to sexual purity. "Because purity isn't an 'until marriage' thing," she said. "I think it's more of an 'until death' sort of thing. Single, married, divorced, same-sex attracted, asexual, whatever. It's a dangerous thing when married sex becomes the 'finish line' for sexual purity."

This can feel overwhelming. Maybe that's one reason Scripture speaks so often about our need for endurance. Maybe it's also why purity rhetoric places such an emphasis on waiting *until* marriage, because the pursuit of purity feels more achievable when there is an end date. But the Bible makes no such promises. We are called to pursue purity until the day we die or Jesus returns, whichever comes first.

But does the pursuit of sexual purity always include virginity? Clearly, there are scenarios where it doesn't—for instance, with someone who has been raped, or someone who was previously married, or someone who is currently married, or someone who has sinned sexually in the past. For many of us, the pursuit of sexual purity *will* include virginity. It did for me until I was twenty-four. But then I got married, and sexual purity meant continuing to try to view people as brothers and sisters in all purity while engaging in the deep and exclusive act of sex with one person, my husband.

After five years of marriage, however, my husband chose to divorce me. At age thirty, I found myself single again. Only this time, I was no longer a virgin. I desperately wanted to honor God by seeking sexual purity, but finding my identity and empowerment in virginity was not possible this time around. I knew that the dating pool would lessen for me now that I was no longer a virgin and carried the baggage of divorce. Not only that, but love had been awakened, as Song of Songs 8:4 talks about, and there was no way to tell it to go back to sleep. My call as a divorced, nonvirgin in her thirties was the same as when I was fourteen or when I was twenty: love God and others with all my heart, mind, body, soul, and strength.

THE SOURCE OF ALL PURITY

Deneson points out that "for three decades, virginity pledges were tallied by the Government Accountability Office as proof of efficacy. Success was loosely measured in ring receipts and course completions, irrespective of the person's actual behavior."[15] And in the same way wearing a purity ring does not guarantee virginity, virginity doesn't guarantee purity.

Virginity is an idol in purity culture that must be dethroned. Dan B. Allender, coauthor of *God Loves Sex*, says that he has "worked with countless men and women who were virgins at marriage, escaped the perversion of pornography, and never kissed their spouse until their wedding day—yet still warred with dark desires or the absence of desire at various periods in their marriage."[16] Virgins or not, Christians are real people who wrestle with sexual temptation. Instead of fixating on virginity, our goal as Christians must be God's glory in our sexual brokenness. The elevation of virginity and the promised reward of great married sex for the chaste not only creates false expectations but makes the pursuit of sexual purity all about personal fulfillment.

Christine Gardner put it best when she said that the solution for evangelicals is not "to value virginity less but to value God more."[17] Too often our elevation of virginity neglects the true source of our purity. The idea that we need to offer nonvirgins some sort of symbolic "second virginity" reinforces our misunderstanding of where purity comes from. We have been made new, washed clean "with the precious blood of Christ, a lamb without blemish or defect" (1 Peter 1:19). Virginity does not provide our purity. Jesus does.

Both sexual sin and abuse come with pain and scars. There are things you'll have to work through, especially if there has been trauma. But you are in no way a less valuable potential spouse, person, or Christian because of what you've done or what's been done to you sexually. Virginity is not required to have a God-honoring life or a healthy marriage. The best gift you can give yourself, your community, or a future spouse is a life surrendered to Christ.

I have heard too many teenagers say: "Well, I've already gone there once. I might as well do it again." Paul must have heard statements like this too because in Romans 6:1 he asks: "What shall we say, then? Shall we go on sinning so that grace may increase?" If we elevate virginity to the point where some feel permanently defeated, then we have ceased to help our brothers and sisters pursue sexual purity.

Not one of us is a crumpled rose, a used car, or an incomplete person. You are a precious image bearer of God. Your purity has already been won for you in Christ, and your dedication to pursuing sexual purity is not defined by your virginity but by your surrender to Christ and dependence on the Holy Spirit *today.* Today is a new day to pursue sexual purity out of love for the God who rescued you and brought you safely to himself in Christ. As Lauren Winner, author of *Real Sex: The Naked Truth About Chastity*, says, when it comes to purity, the most important question to ask is not, what have I done but, what am I doing now?[18]

DISCUSSION QUESTIONS

1. Did you experience any purity demonstrations, like passing a rose around the room, when you were young? If so, how did they affect you? What do you think of such metaphors now?
2. Is virginity the best gift a person can give their spouse? Why or why not?
3. What are your thoughts on government-funded abstinence education?
4. Is there a place for purity rings, necklaces, and pledge cards?
5. How does sexual sin affect marriage? How can we talk about sexual sin in a healthy, biblical way?
6. How would you define sexual purity?
7. If you ever have children, how will you talk about virginity with your child?

ACTIVITY

Take some time to finish these sentences individually. If you're having trouble answering them for yourself, try answering them based on what you would want your child to be able to say about themselves. After everyone is finished, go around and share some of your responses.

I have value because:________________________

When God sees me, he sees:____________________

My sins are:______________________________

My commitment to sexual purity today looks like:________

3

FEMALE RESPONSIBILITIES

From an early age, Cassie saw her body as a stumbling block to men. She lived out in the country with her family, was homeschooled, and went back and forth between a charismatic church with her parents and a Baptist church with her grandparents. The influence of Bill Gothard filled her home. And at age thirteen, she was sexually assaulted by a man in church.

She went home that day and considered cutting off her breasts—as though they were the problem. As though *she* were the problem. Her very femaleness felt like a weapon that she had no desire to wield. Cassie told her parents what had happened. They talked to church leadership. Nothing happened. And so the story goes. On and on, over and over again.

THE "MORAL SUPERIORITY OF WOMEN"

Women are often portrayed as gullible and easily tempted. But modern purity culture places them on a pedestal of self-control. It says that men and women are "defined primarily by their biological instincts," and that women are less tempted by sex.[1] This idea, coupled with teachings about the insatiable nature of male lust, sets women up as the guardians of sexual purity.

Evangelical thought leaders like Dr. James Dobson talk about how women have a civilizing effect on men. Dobson preaches the importance of marriage as "the cornerstone of civilization," believing that it is in marriage that women civilize their husbands. Moslener notes a connection between Dobson's views and the work of George Gilder, a "conservative, antifeminist." According to Gilder, men need women because they are barbarians who can only succeed if women balance out their aggressive tendencies.[2] In both Dobson's and Gilder's views, it is the duty of women to keep men in check.

These ideas might sound like a nod of respect to women, but they actually place an impossible weight on their shoulders. And ultimately, Moslener points out, the idea of female moral superiority has led to increased "monitoring and control of female sexuality."[3]

FEMALE SEXUALITY DOWNPLAYED

These ideas are built, in part, on the assumption that women are less sexual than men. I picked up on this stereotype from a young age, noticing how the wives in sitcoms were always rolling their eyes at their husband's desire for intimacy and saying with annoyance, "Not tonight." I remember hearing women from church talk often about the importance of being sexually available to your husband, as though it were a duty or a chore rather than something they wanted. I remember blushing at my desire and wondering if I was some sort of outlier.

Purity conferences also deemphasized female sexuality. Events for teenage boys portrayed lust as "a basic element in what it means to be a male," while those for young women discussed topics like modesty and guarding your heart.[4] Joshua Harris, too, assumed that "girls don't struggle with the same temptations" men do.[5] Other books for Christian men, like *Wild at Heart* and *Every Man's Battle*, claim that women are not as sexually aroused by visual stimuli.[6] And while men are given plenty of advice about how to avoid lust, and women are taught how to help them, there is little to no advice for men about how to help *women* avoid lust.

We need not erase the differences between the sexes to prove that women are sexual. When God created woman, he designed her body to include erogenous zones that have no bearing on reproduction and serve only one purpose: female sexual pleasure. Men and women are different, but they are both sexual beings. Purity culture may downplay this, but Scripture does not. The bride speaking in the opening of Song of Songs describes her desires:

> Let him kiss me with the kisses of his mouth!
> For your love is better than wine;
> your anointing oils are fragrant;
> your name is oil poured out;
> therefore virgins love you.
> Draw me after you; let us run.
> The king has brought me into his chambers.
> (Song of Songs 1:1-4 ESV)

Whatever your theological approach to Song of Songs, sexual expression inside marriage is celebrated here. And it is undeniable that this desire crosses gender lines. The bride wants her husband—his body, his kisses, and his bed. This desire is God-given, and Scripture celebrates it. In her book *Love Thy Body*, Nancy Pearcey drew my attention to Deuteronomy 24:5, which states: "If a man has recently married, he must not be sent to war or have any other duty laid on him. For one year he is to be free to stay at home and bring happiness to the wife he has married." Here, Pearcey notes, is "an astonishing departure from the low view of women in the surrounding polytheistic cultures," as young husbands are encouraged to focus their energy on pleasing their new wives.[7] In the Bible women are depicted as able to experience sexual joy and pleasure.

WHAT WOMEN ARE TAUGHT

Despite the reality of female sexual desire, purity books for women only occasionally address lust. Instead, they focus on women's responsibilities to wait for marriage, guard their hearts and bodies for their future husband, protect male purity, attract the right mate, and keep their husband sexually satisfied. It's a lot.

An overwhelming number of Christian books on purity, dating, and singleness were written for women in the late 1990s and early 2000s. I have chosen eight of them that demonstrate the range of teachings for women during this era. Some of the ideas will have you nodding your head in agreement, maybe even clapping and saying amen, while others may shock you, cause you to cringe, or perhaps make you want to throw this book across the room. All reactions are welcome—just make sure to keep reading, as later chapters will address these ideas in greater depth.

When I was a teenager, Christian singer and Grammy award winner Rebecca St. James turned her song about purity, "Wait for Me," into a larger conversation about how Christians can honor God and their future spouse by remaining sexually abstinent before marriage. In her book *Wait for Me: Rediscovering the Power of Purity in Romance* (2002), St. James says that waiting well begins with restoring one's dream of being a princess "rescued by a knight" and guarding one's heart, mind, and body for marriage.[8] In her popular song, "Wait for Me," she sings about waiting for her future love, praying for him, and hoping that he will "hold on" and keep his "loving eyes" only for her.[9]

A few years earlier, author and missionary Elisabeth Elliot wrote *Let Me Be a Woman: Notes to My Daughter on the Meaning of Womanhood* (1999) to help her daughter, Valerie, understand the differences between men and women. John and Stasi Eldredge also wrote about femininity and the desires of a woman's heart in *Captivating: Unveiling the Mystery of a Woman's Soul* (2011), believing that their book could help set women free.[10]

Dannah Gresh wrote *And the Bride Wore White: Seven Secrets to Sexual Purity* (2012) to help women pursue sexual purity and move forward from sexual sin. With a similar goal, Shannon Ethridge and Stephen Arterburn coauthored *Every Young Woman's Battle: Guarding Your Mind, Heart, and Body in a Sex-Saturated World,* hoping to help women navigate the desires of their hearts and bodies.[11] Unlike many books written for Christian women, Arterburn and Ethridge broach topics such as masturbation, sexual abuse, and pornography, acknowledging that sexual lust is not a male-specific problem.

For those seeking marriage, Eric and Leslie Ludy present an alternative to casual dating in their book *Romance God's Way* (1997) and Sarah Mally, author of *Before You Meet Prince Charming* (2006), promotes courtship, the idea that young women should remain under the protection of their parents, especially their fathers, until marriage.[12]

Shaunti Feldhahn, a graduate of Harvard University and a former analyst on Wall Street, along with author and screenwriter Lisa A. Rice, wrote *For Young Women Only: What You Need to Know About How Guys Think* (2006), using data gathered from informal interviews with young men, as well as a "scientific survey of four hundred guys from all over the country who were between the ages of fifteen and twenty."[13] Their desire is to help young women understand what young men are looking for.

Most of the advice for young Christian women has to do with waiting. Mally's entire book centers around waiting and preparing for marriage, with the assumption that most women will get married and the belief that being a wife and mother are "the calling God has for [women's] lives."[14] Elliot, too, believes that "most women marry" and that the stage of singleness can be a gift.[15] In every book, singleness is emphasized as a *temporary* season of waiting when women can prepare for marriage by learning patience, practicing self-control, and developing into a godly potential spouse.

Like Elliot, the Eldredges see waiting as a gift because it gives women the chance to look to "the face of God."[16] Women, they say, become beautiful when they know they are loved. The Eldredges encourage women to view God not just as the Lord they worship at church, but as a "pursuer" and "lover," and Jesus as the one who can truly satisfy their deepest longings.[17] Arterburn and Ethridge echo this, pointing out that "true beauty . . . radiates from a heart that delights in the Lord."[18]

Some women shared with me that they were encouraged to go on dates with Jesus and to imagine him putting on a tuxedo and whisking them onto the dance floor for a dip and a kiss. Others declared "Jesus is my boyfriend" so they could feel like they were a part of a couple without the pitfalls and temptations of dating. The idea that Christ alone satisfies is biblical. Jesus *should* be the love of our life, regardless of our gender or marital status. But aspects of this rhetoric seem to cheapen Jesus rather than honor him, especially when he is treated as a stand-in—a buffer—to keep young women emotionally and physically pure until their dream guy shows up. Jesus is indeed the lover of our souls. He is the bridegroom of the church. But he is not a chameleon who changes color to match the current shade of our longing.

WHAT WOMEN MUST GUARD

Arterburn and Ethridge view singleness as a time when women must wage war against temptation by guarding their minds, hearts, and bodies.[19] This rhetoric of guarding emphasizes female responsibility, the task of creating and maintaining physical boundaries. Despite the references in so many of these books make to brave knights protecting and rescuing princesses, Arterburn and Ethridge tell young women, "Remember, no one else can guard your body and your sexual purity. That's your job."[20]

The mind. While visual temptation isn't addressed nearly as often in books for Christian women as it is for men, St. James does include a letter in her book from a teenage girl who admits to being addicted to pornography. She suggests that Christian singles put on "spiritual blinders" to keep impure thoughts and images out.[21] Arterburn and Ethridge also acknowledge that women can be visually tempted, encouraging those who look at pornography to flee the habit if they want to achieve "sexual integrity and spiritual peace."[22] While the subject deserves a more thorough discussion than these books provide, it is encouraging that some of them address visual temptation for women.

But the majority of advice for women about guarding the mind has to do with "emotional fantasy."[23] After the Fifty Shades of Grey series came out, Dannah Gresh and Dr. Julianna Slattery wrote a book called *Pulling Back the Shades,* where they warned women to avoid reading the series because it "has done for women and erotica what the advent of the Internet did for men and porn."[24] In other words, romance novels can be just as dangerous to the cause of mental purity as viewing pornography.

The heart. The reverberating advice of my youth came from a section of Proverbs 4:23 that tells the Christian, "Guard your heart." I don't remember this verse being exposited or the context explained. It took on a meaning of its own when applied to adolescent dating: namely, that young Christians should be careful with their emotions when interacting with the opposite sex. I was warned against spending too much time with any one boy or having conversations that went too deep. Rebecca Lemke writes about hearing a similar message, noting that crushes were depicted as "the equivalent of an emotional STD."[25]

Purity culture places a significant focus on women guarding their hearts before marriage. Mally's book, for instance, has an entire chapter titled "Guard Your Heart," and this oft-repeated advice seems to be built on the assumption that a woman's desire for emotional intimacy often leads to physical intimacy.[26] Because they believe women are "emotionally stimulated," Arterburn and Ethridge conclude that the battle for sexual purity begins in the heart.[27] Leslie Ludy says that after dating multiple men, she realized that her "heart was a treasure" she wanted to guard for her future husband.[28] The Ludys encourage single Christians to be faithful to their future spouse not just physically but also emotionally.[29]

The authors have different advice about what "guarding the heart" means in practice. Mally uses the metaphor of a cake with a piece cut out to illustrate a woman who has given away part of her heart before marriage.[30] To remain whole, Mally suggests that women avoid sharing "personal or intimate things with [their] guy friends," treat men as acquaintances, and try to keep conversations with them brief.[31] For Gresh, dating that is "safe for the heart" is careful not to rush certain things.[32] When she was dating the man who would become her husband, Gresh decided not to discuss marriage or sex specifically until after he proposed marriage.[33]

The body. In most of these books, the problematic messages are tangled up with biblical wisdom. But when it comes to what the authors tell women about guarding their bodies, I found landmine after landmine. In her book, Mally says that a "pure white rose" can "tear" and be "lost or damaged forever" if someone tries to open it too soon, or if it is "handled and played with by too many a fellow."[34] Mally believes that men are less likely to "take advantage of girls they respect," and Gresh believes that a woman is unlikely to find herself in a "compromising situation" if she sets proper physical boundaries.[35]

"Kristy should have known better than to be alone with Daniel behind closed doors," Arterburn and Ethridge write. Women are expected to understand that certain actions, such as flirting, kissing, or lying horizontally with a man, can make them a "sexual target."[36] Arterburn wants young women to know that even Christian men fall into using women for sex and that, each time they do, they take "a piece of her soul." Arterburn and Ethridge go so far as to include a five-point list of "practical ways to avoid being sexually abused or raped," advising women to "stay in relatively public places" and to refrain from engaging "in sexually arousing behaviors" on dates.[37] Gresh tells women to be careful about where they go, encouraging them to avoid any places where they are truly alone with a man because a princess should "stay within the confines of her own kingdom," where others can see and protect her.[38]

As for conduct on dates, Feldhahn and Rice conclude from their research that "many guys don't feel the ability or the responsibility to stop the sexual progression" with a date.[39] I asked various women about this idea, wondering if they had also noticed it. The majority agreed that the expectation, even if unspoken, is that they are responsible for setting the physical boundaries in their dating relationships. A young woman named Morgan said that her ex-boyfriend always seemed willing to go further sexually than she wanted to, so she had to communicate which lines she wasn't willing to cross.

Almost every author takes the time to address and give some hope to those who have sinned sexually. Gresh reminds her readers that people are born sinners and that purity is more about "where you end up."[40] Mally tells women who feel they have "already messed up" that there is healing and forgiveness at the cross, and even the possibility of future happiness in marriage.[41] St. James believes that although many people feel "deep sadness" when they have premarital sex, a fresh start is still possible because virginity is not just a physical state but "an attitude, a way of thinking."[42]

But alongside these encouragements are warnings. Lots of warnings. The authors talk about how sexual promiscuity can lead to sexually transmitted diseases, infertility, and the "inability to enjoy sex" with one's future spouse.[43] Arterburn and Ethridge ask their female readers, "Do you want to live to walk down the aisle at your wedding someday?" and proceed to discuss the dangers of STDs to the body and to a woman's fertility.[44] Gresh, too, discusses the potential of "no babies . . . ever" for women who are sexually active outside of marriage.[45]

Some of the authors provide brief passages directly addressing those who have been sexually abused. St. James encourages those who have had their purity "stolen away" through abuse to begin "processing the pain" rather than living in silence and guilt.[46] Gresh echoes this advice, telling victims that what happened to them "was not [their] fault."[47]

Although they plead with those who have been sexually abused to seek help and healing, the authors also warn them that abuse can open the door to sexual promiscuity.[48] Stasi Eldredge shares that she was raped and describes how it produced in her a "sense of shame and self-loathing."[49] Arterburn and Ethridge tell three different stories of women who were sexually assaulted and then became promiscuous to numb their pain or "regain a sense of control."[50] Whether or not this connection is valid, sexual abuse appears more as a vehicle to continue to discuss sexual immorality rather than a distinct subject that deserves its own discussion.

WHAT WOMEN MUST DO

Dress modestly. One of the most controversial topics in purity culture is female modesty. In purity literature, women are taught to be aware of how their actions, glances, and dress could inspire male lust.[51] Elliot believes that modesty was at one time "a system of protection."[52] St. James speaks about it in the same way, exhorting young women to dress modestly if they "don't want to be treated poorly or like an object."[53] The pressure on women to guard the purity of both genders through modesty is presented not as a burden but as a form of empowerment.[54] According to Gresh, modesty has an "intoxicating" influence over men and can be an "untapped power source" for women.[55] It creates a "positive 'obstacle'" which motivates men to "invest into your life in order to one day enjoy your allure."[56]

Harris pleads with young women to be mindful of the impact their clothing choices have on men, acknowledging that "yes, guys are responsible for maintaining self-control," but women can "help" men by wearing modest outfits.[57] Gresh says that men were made to "physically yearn" for women's bodies and the way women act and dress can be "explosive fuels."[58] And Feldhahn and Rice believe that women who cover up their bodies are less likely to be sexually tempting to men.[59]

Arterburn and Ethridge illustrate similar beliefs, telling the story of Rachel who "started dressing more provocatively" and one day was unable to get a man to stop kissing her, even after asking him to stop. "He said there was no way I could expect him to take no for an answer after everything I had been saying to him to drive him crazy," Rachel recalls. The only commentary they add to this story is to note how Rachel "realized that it's no innocent game to behave seductively."[60]

I will never forget the day, during my time teaching at a private Christian high school, that a group of my female students gathered around my desk with furrowed brows and a flood of questions after having been told by another teacher: "You are responsible for the purity of men." It was picture day, so the girls were not wearing their uniforms but rather dresses and skirts that made them feel beautiful. Some of their skirts were shorter than usual, and this had prompted a gender-segregated speech on modesty by my coworker. Instead of feeling empowered by the idea that their dress had such influence over their male classmates, their shoulders slumped under the weight of the responsibility placed on them.

Lemke says that, growing up, she often felt she was just "a stray bra strap away" from causing one of her male friends to sin or sexually assault her.[61] I, too, remember feeling guilty if I discovered that a shirt I had worn fit looser than I thought and that, when I bent over, I might have caused someone to sin. Despite being flat-chested and plain, summer season often made me feel more like a potential stumbling block than a young girl excited to go to the beach. I always remembered to put shorts on over my swimsuit and to wear a swim cover when I wasn't in the water.

The rhetoric is confusing to young women. Are men brave princes, or are they dragons that must be tamed? Or maybe *women* are the dragons. Klein says: "Imagine growing up in a castle and hearing fables about how dragons destroy villages and kill good people all your life. Then, one day, you wake up and see scales on your arms and legs and realize . . . *I* am a dragon."[62] The fairy tale falls apart. We look at our bodies and feel ashamed.

As many women who grew up in purity culture will tell you, at some point the rhetoric of modesty begins to feel less about being wise and selfless and more about the sin of having a female body. Multiple women shared with me that, because of their shape, it doesn't seem to matter what they wear—they get confronted. A woman with large breasts, for example, will continue to have large breasts whether she wears a turtleneck or a tank top. In purity rhetoric, modesty is too often determined by how naturally attractive or shapely a woman is rather than what she chooses to wear and the heart attitude behind it. Beauty becomes the sin, not immodesty.

Women of color often experience this in a more pronounced way. As Jasmine Holmes points out, black women are oversexualized in America, having been freed from slavery only to discover that femininity and purity "had been defined in their absence."[63] Alia Joy talks about the tension she felt as a young Asian-American girl who "longed for blond hair and blue eyes and a name like Jennifer or Melissa or Sarah," only to grow into a woman who had to face the fetishization of Asian women in America.[64] She recalls the whispers and cat-calls: "'I've got Yellow Fever,' they joke . . . as I walk by. Their labels slither serpentine down my hips, all venom and fangs and poison so strong it takes me years to believe myself anything but nasty."[65]

One of the main problems with modesty rhetoric is that it draws on the biblically unsupportable idea that women are responsible for the purity of men. If a man lusts after a woman, it is because she failed to protect him. Going further, if a man sexually assaults a woman, the question is often asked not only by campus security guards but by those in the church: "What was she wearing when it happened?" When modesty rhetoric confuses culpability, consistently blaming women for the actions of men, we have ceased to be biblical in our approach. I interviewed a young Christian husband who pointed out that while "there is biblical wisdom in teaching people to dress in a modest way," the discussion should "not be restricted to one gender." He added, "a woman can be incredibly modest, but if my desires are leading me to seek out sinful satisfaction, I'm going to find it, regardless of what they're wearing."

The concept of female moral superiority is neither biblical nor helpful to the discussion of modesty. Men and women are equally able to resist sexual temptation: "No temptation has overtaken you that is not common to man. God is faithful, and he will not let you be tempted beyond your ability, but with the temptation he will also provide the way of escape, that you may be able to endure it" (1 Corinthians 10:13 ESV). What we must remember in the modesty debate is that believers are held accountable to God for their individual actions. Jesus clearly taught that men are responsible for their own lust: "But I tell you that anyone who looks at a woman lustfully has already committed adultery with her in his heart" (Matthew 5:28).

No one gets to blame someone else for their own sin. A man can't say that a woman's short skirt made him lust any more than a woman can blame a man's shirtless gym pic on Instagram for making her masturbate. Likewise, a man or woman who intentionally dresses to attract sexual lust from a brother or sister in Christ will be held accountable for that selfishness and lack of love. We are individually responsible for our sins. Romans 14:12 says that "each of us will give an account of ourselves to God."

Despite the unbiblical arguments, modesty *is* a biblical concept and we need to learn how to talk about it rightly. In 1 Peter 3, women learn that modesty is less about dressing up the outside and more about the inner person and "the unfading beauty of a gentle and quiet spirit" (v. 4). Peter goes on to explain what this means, pointing to how the "holy women of the past who put their hope in God" (v. 5) submitted to their own husbands and were fearless. Here having a quiet heart does not mean remaining silent. It means being brave and hushing the fearful voices inside our hearts.

Timothy also addresses female modesty (1 Timothy 2:9-10), reminding women that true adornment is pursuing good works, not fixing their hair or showing off their wealth. He addresses what women wear, noting that it should be respectable and discreet. But respectable dress is determined by one's cultural context. We can and should make a point of understanding what is considered modest and humble for the context we are in, whether we are on a mission trip to Africa, on vacation in China, or at a church picnic in North America.

One woman told me that when she visited Africa, she left her shorts at home and wore long skirts that covered her ankles. She didn't worry so much about bringing shirts with high necklines. In certain parts of Africa, legs are viewed as sexually appealing whereas breasts are more utilitarian. Women regularly breastfeed in public, without covers. Another friend who works with Muslim refugees in the United States told me that she is careful to wear pants and long-sleeved shirts that cover her buttocks, especially around men. She has also stopped running outside in her neighborhood, as most athletic gear is too tight and she is determined to love her Muslim neighbors, including but not limited to the way she dresses around them.

What if we took the same care that we take in loving people from other cultures through our dress in our own culture? In our local church? We are often more willing to dress modestly when we are pursuing missionary work somewhere else or with people in different cultural contexts than we are in our own communities and churches—as though our whole lives are not meant to be a light for the gospel, or as though the people in our small group at church are less important than the people we ministered to last summer in Mexico. Our call to love one another doesn't take vacation days, and loving our neighbors includes thinking about how we dress.

We don't have the freedom to judge others based on dress, but we *do* have the freedom to consider them in how we dress. One way we sin against God and our neighbor is by being self-centered with our Christian freedom. Romans 14 discusses the tension in the early church between those who felt free to consume meat that had been sacrificed to idols and those who felt convicted that they should refrain from eating it. In this one passage, we are reminded of a few important things that could help us regarding our discussions about modesty:

> You, then, why do you judge your brother or sister? Or why do you treat them with contempt? For we will all stand before God's judgment seat. It is written:
>
> "'As surely as I live,' says the Lord,
> 'every knee will bow before me;
> every tongue will acknowledge God.'"
>
> So then, each of us will give an account of ourselves to God. Therefore let us stop passing judgment on one another. Instead, make up your mind not to put any stumbling block or obstacle in the way of a brother or sister. (Romans 14:10-13)

It is not our job to judge the motives of one who eats meat or wears yoga pants. It *is* our job to consider our own actions and how well they fulfill the first and second greatest commandment from Jesus to love God and love others. We don't get to blame someone else for our sexual sin. Neither do we get to be careless or selfish in how we dress. "You, my brothers and sisters, were called to be free. But do not use your freedom to indulge the flesh; rather, serve one another humbly in love" (Galatians 5:13).

Select a spouse. The Eldredges believe that every woman wants to feel they are someone "worth pursuing."[66] Despite this supposed universal desire, Christian books put the responsibility on women to sort through the "toads" to find a "prince."[67] It is worth noting that, in each of these books, heterosexual attraction is assumed, leaving women who experience same-sex attraction out of the conversation. Gresh encourages women to "dream of someone who is just right" by creating a list of attributes they want in their future spouse and claims that she never went on a second date with a man who failed to meet the criteria on her list.[68]

The "list" was quite the trend when I was in high school. Almost all my friends had one, right down to eye color and taste in music. These lists became household idols for some of us. We held them up beside each boy we met, measuring their worth in bullet points. The perfect husband existed on paper alone, and we spent hours daydreaming about him. In contrast, Elliot reminds her daughter that, in looking for a spouse, "there's nobody else to marry" but another sinner, and women must be ready to accept their husbands, love them, and forgive them as they have been forgiven by God.[69]

Attract a spouse. Paired with advice about what to look for in a mate are suggestions about how to attract one. "To be rescued, one must first be a princess," Mally says.[70] According to Gresh, a princess does not wear her heart on her sleeve because men have an "insatiable need" to chase, earn, and win the affection of a woman.[71] Elliot echoes this advice, encouraging her daughter to "leave room for mystery."[72] It is those women who know when to be guarded and reserved who are "respected by men," Mally says.[73] I remember reading similar advice and sighing with disappointment, knowing that I was too transparent to be mysterious and too loud to be seen as reserved.

The Eldredges believe that feminine beauty is inviting, not demanding.[74] Men are looking for women who will show them respect and admiration, according to Feldhahn and Rice.[75] While they briefly remark that it is important not to ignore "obvious concerns" in a relationship, they tell young women that men need to be respected unconditionally "for who they are, apart from how they do," and they suggest that if women want to be someone men "gravitate toward," they should give men compliments instead of nagging or correcting them.[76] Elliot encourages her daughter that it is not necessarily about telling him "how wonderful he is" but about sincerely appreciating "those qualities that you originally saw and admired" in him.[77]

In one chapter, the Eldredges tell the story of a WWII soldier who, after being tended to by a female nurse, asked to watch her put on her lipstick because female beauty "soothes the soul."[78] They believe that it is "true femininity" which "arouses true masculinity."[79] Feldhahn and Rice say that men want to be with women who are confident, take care of themselves, and are a "healthy weight."[80] One man told them that he knew a girl who could be attractive if she "tried a little harder," while others suggested that women make the connection between their lack of dates and being "twenty or thirty pounds over a healthy weight."[81]

Satisfy her spouse. The deemphasis on female sexual desire might be one reason that purity culture rhetoric places such a focus on male sexual fulfillment in marriage. Because men are portrayed as "always in the mood" for sex, women are the ones encouraged to satisfy their spouses sexually. They are advised to provide regular sexual release for their husbands "without complaint" because "the Bible says you should not withhold sex for long periods of time."[82] Being sexually giving in marriage is certainly biblical, but these authors miss the fact that Paul's words in 1 Corinthians 7 are for both wives *and* husbands.

Alongside this lopsided emphasis on male sexual fulfillment, there is pressure and responsibility placed on Christian wives to help their husbands fight sexual sin by giving them sex. One woman writes that even if a wife does not feel she has the time or energy for sex with her husband, if she truly cares "about his purity" she will muster up just what it takes "to get him by." Even when a husband has broken trust with his wife by sinning sexually, she is called to help her husband quit his sexual sin by increasing her "availability to him sexually."[83]

Wives are called to "be like a merciful vial of methadone" for their husbands who are battling sexual lust, regardless of the chasm sexual sin creates or the feelings of betrayal they may be experiencing.

This overemphasis on a wife's responsibility to give her husband sex creates an attitude of expectation that could open the door to sexual abuse within marriage. If a woman is not providing enough sexual release for her husband, he might consider it his right to seek it by force, or outside the marriage. Sadly, these messages mark wives as sexual outlets rather than equal sexual partners.

COMPLICATIONS WITH FEMALE RESPONSIBILITIES

As I studied these books, I noticed that the authors often lump the sexually immoral and sexually abused together. The Eldredges' "prayer for sexual healing" includes those who have sinned and those who feel broken due to abuse.[84] Likewise, the call for women to guard themselves—mind, body, and soul—is communicated as a way to guard against sexual sin *and* sexual abuse. In fact, Mally's book includes a drawing of a princess who has been turned into black soot by a fire-breathing dragon and the caption under the image says, "Anxious maidens must not play with fire-breathing dragons lest they be burnt."[85] The underlying message in these books is that women should set boundaries not only to protect themselves from their own temptations but from being sinned against.

This repeated call for women to guard their hearts and bodies can make abuse seem like the result of a woman's failure to set sufficient boundaries. Women are warned against dressing, flirting, and smiling in ways that attract male attention.[86] If a woman "passionately kisses" a man, according to Arterburn and Ethridge, she is communicating that she can be treated like "his little plaything," but if she sets the right boundaries, she teaches men her value; that she "is worth the wait." Women are warned against "stirring up desires" within men, and Feldhahn and Rice tell women that men "need you to help protect both of you." If a man continues to disrespect a woman's boundaries, she is advised to tell him and "get offensive if necessary." The message these authors communicate—that "you teach people how to treat you"—assumes that if a woman experiences nonconsensual sexual activity, it is her fault because she had the power and responsibility to prevent it.[87]

Even advice to women about how to attract a mate morphs into a complicated rhetoric of responsibility. Feldhahn and Rice advise women to consider how much men desire respect from them, telling them to "watch for [his] anger," if they want to know when they have "crossed the disrespect line," and that if they are respectful and polite to men, "everything will open up" for them.[88] In all of this advice about sexual boundaries, modest dress, and making men feel respected, Christian women are told that it is within their control to be treated with dignity and attract a quality mate, which also means that if a man mistreats them or if they are unable to find a suitable mate, they share part of the blame. What a heavy weight of false guilt we place on women's shoulders with these messages!

It follows too that, if a relationship fails, the woman must share the blame. Maybe she stopped wearing makeup and "let herself go." Maybe she wasn't sexually pleasing enough. When my ex-husband was in the process of divorcing me, a Christian man reached out and told me that my husband would surely come back if I put on my prettiest dress, knocked on his door, and told him I was sorry. In one confrontation, this man summarized my worst fears. Although my ex-husband told me that he was divorcing me because we no longer shared the same faith, my insecurity often causes me to wonder if he really left because of some lack in my beauty or personality.

I have heard the question asked, in hushed tones, after a man cheats on his wife: "Why did he feel the need to go outside the marriage?" The implication is that his wife could have stopped his sin—she is partially responsible. Instead of teaching individual responsibility for sexual sin, purity teachings often turn wives into coguardians of their husband's sexual purity. When her husband began cheating on her with multiple women, church leaders asked a close friend of mine, "What did you do that led him to this behavior?" If women are expected to have a civilizing effect on men as purity culture teaches, then it is only reasonable to assume that when a husband acts uncivilized, his wife is at least partially responsible.

Barbara shared her story with Justin and Lindsey Holcomb: "When I told him to stop or that I was in pain, he ignored my pleas, told me to be quiet, or argued that I was to be submissive. . . . For many years I didn't see what was happening as rape."[89] Women experience "intimate partner violence" more than any other form of violence, with it affecting "30% of women worldwide."[90] Barbara rationalized his behavior, unable to admit that her own husband was raping her. Instead of reaching out for help, she became isolated from others, obsessed with being "the model wife," and dealt with thoughts like, "I should have known better than to marry him," and "I should have seen this coming."[91]

Teachings about the moral superiority and responsibility of women place a burden on them that Scripture does not. The rhetoric reduces women to their sexual function, instead of depicting them the way Scripture does, as image bearers of God and coheirs of the kingdom. The idea that women can prevent disrespect and sexual harassment simply by dressing and acting in certain ways is not only unbiblical and statistically inaccurate, it is dangerous and often leads to false blame for female victims of abuse. What might appear as respect for the female gender is actually an oppressive standard that assumes women can control the actions of men. Such "empowerment" leaves women feeling defeated and guilty, rather than valued by the church and strengthened in Christ.

DISCUSSION QUESTIONS

1. Did you read any of the books mentioned in this chapter? If so, how did they affect you?
2. Do you believe women are more responsible for maintaining sexual boundaries than men? Why or why not?
3. What does it mean to guard our hearts? In what ways have we interpreted this biblically, and in what ways have we gone beyond Scripture?
4. Do you agree with Mally that men are less likely to "take advantage of girls they respect"? Why or why not?
5. Should churches have dress codes or modesty rules? Why or why not?
6. What do you think about "the list"—writing down what you want in a future spouse?
7. What do you think about the emphasis placed on male sexual fulfillment in marriage, and the silence on female sexual desire?

ACTIVITY

Read Romans 14:15-21 and try replacing "what you eat" with "what you wear," and "eating and drinking" with a piece of clothing that would be considered controversial or a flaunting of wealth in your cultural context. Have someone read the passage aloud.

If your brother or sister is distressed because of what you [wear], you are no longer acting in love. Do not by your [clothing] destroy someone for whom Christ died. Therefore do not let what you know is good be spoken of as evil. For the kingdom of God is not a matter of [whether or not one wears ______________], but of righteousness, peace and joy in the Holy Spirit, because anyone who serves Christ in this way is pleasing to God and receives human approval. Let us therefore make every effort to do what leads to peace and to mutual edification. Do not destroy the work of God for the sake of [clothing]. All [clothing] is clean, but it is wrong for a person to [wear] anything that causes someone else to stumble. It is better not to [wear ________________] or to do anything else that will cause your brother or sister to fall.

4

MALE PURITY AND THE RHETORIC OF LUST

Mike Pence, current vice president of the United States, has been criticized for adhering to what is called the "Billy Graham rule." The idea, taken from Graham's decision never to travel or meet with women alone, is a topic worth discussing. Does such a rule respect women or degrade them? Is it worth limiting opportunities for women in ministry and the workplace if following the rule helps men stay faithful to their wives? Whatever your views, this rule is a microcosm of the teachings directed at Christian men in modern purity culture. Men are primarily taught that they are lust machines and that the key to battling sexual sin is to avoid images, places, and women who might inspire it.

WHAT MEN WERE TAUGHT

To illustrate what men were taught in the modern purity era, I will dig into the themes from three bestselling Christian books written by men, popular in the late 1990s and early 2000s: *Wild at Heart* by John Eldredge (2001), *I Kissed Dating Goodbye* by Joshua Harris (1997), and *Every Man's Battle* by Stephen Arterburn and Fred Stoeker (2000). These were the books I saw my male friends reading in high school. *Wild at Heart* sold over one million copies, and it seemed like almost every young Christian man had a copy of *Every Man's Battle* on his bookshelf. Parents bought their sons these books for graduation gifts, and they were selected for men's Bible studies. Their influence should not be underestimated.

If you want to understand John Eldredge's view of manhood in *Wild at Heart,* picture a Patagonia ad with an unshaven man in hiking gear, and there you have it. According to Eldredge, the problem is not that men "don't know how to keep their promises, be spiritual leaders, talk to their wives, or raise their children," but that they have been disallowed freedom and adventure.[1] He encourages men to explore their wild strength and to "stop being a nice guy and act like a warrior."[2] In *Every Man's Battle,* Arterburn and Stoeker focus on self-control as manliness. They use wartime imagery to communicate practical strategies Christian men can employ to fight sexual lust.[3] Harris also touches on the battle against lust, depicting purity as an all-encompassing pursuit which involves one's motivations, mind, and heart.[4]

BRAVE KNIGHTS

In her research on modern purity culture, Gardner observes that battle metaphors are "common in abstinence rhetoric," especially in messages directed at young men.[5] Harris, Eldredge, and Arterburn and Stoeker all use terms such as *warrior, knight,* and *battle* in their descriptions of manhood and discussions about sexual purity.[6] Even in St. James's book, the knight must defeat "countless bloodthirsty creatures" and travel through a "swamp and forest" to make it to his princess.[7] According to Eldredge, this is what every man longs for: an adventure, "a battle to fight . . . and a beauty to rescue."[8] As with the books written for women, only heterosexual attraction is acknowledged. These masculine images tell men to harness their bravery and strength to fight against sexual lust and win the heart of their princess.

While this might inspire some men, the medieval knight meets outdoorsy daredevil image doesn't appeal to all males. According to one man I interviewed, the church put masculinity in a box too narrow. It was all "sports metaphors" and "let's be pushy and go camping," he told me. "How will you approach biblical masculinity with your son?" I asked. He paused, then said:

> Scripture allows for a man to be himself—to have the kind of personality God has given him. I am not the gruff hunter type of man—that's just not my personality. And for a very long time I've struggled with feeling "manly." There were times that I played volleyball in high school, but I also sang. I want to teach my kids the roles that Scripture lays out for them—focus primarily on that—and then give them the gospel and encourage them that their personality doesn't limit their gender role.

SEX MACHINES?

During my research, I interviewed Blake and John, both husbands and fathers from different churches and backgrounds, who were full of honest questions, feedback, and zeal to see the church grow in her approach to sexual purity. It did my heart good to talk to these brothers. At one point our conversation turned to the reality of sexual rejection in marriage. Only this time, it wasn't about how wives don't give their husband enough sex but about women who feel sexually rejected by their husbands—something I have never heard addressed at any conference or in any book.

"I went into my marriage with certain expectations," Blake told us. "Things people were telling me, like men crave sex six times more than women do."

"Where did you hear that?" I asked him.

"One of the megachurch pastors was on stage with his wife and they were breaking it down." He continued: "A wife might think her husband is looking at pornography, when really, maybe he just had a long day and if you sit still long enough, you're going to fall asleep."

We all laughed. I thought about times I've interpreted my husband's tiredness as rejection and other women who have shared similar experiences. It is a deep pain, pressed deeper still by the stereotype that men always want sex. Women wonder if there is something wrong with their body, their perfume, or their performance in bed. They wrack their brains to figure out what *they* are doing wrong. Shouldn't their husband always want them?

John chimed in, "Just look at the commercials on TV when you're watching sports. They're telling me I need to take this pill so I can be constantly sexually active."

"That's a lot of pressure," I said.

"Yeah," he said, "and it's a prototypical, narrow-minded view about what it means to be a man." I asked him what he wished women knew going forward. "I think maybe changing the definition from 'men are obsessed with sex' to 'men are immersed in sex,'" he said. "The church culture almost reinforces it, making all the instructions about masculinity about sex. We are immersed in this sexual culture and we limit the focus of Christianity for men to getting a job, being good at sex in marriage, and lifting lots of weights. That's the biblical masculinity we're often taught."

Unlike the way they're portrayed in sitcoms and Christian books, men are human beings, not sex machines. They are embodied. Health, age, depression, past abuse, and daily life can all affect their sex drive. A husband's love for his wife is not determined by his libido. A marriage is not in jeopardy simply because the couple has sex less frequently than another couple. If you are a husband or wife feeling sexually rejected, do not despair. Talk to your spouse, but also talk to God. Tell him your hurt, your fears, and your desires. Admit the stereotypes you've fallen for, the ones that have skewed your expectations. Lay them down at his feet. We are complex, embodied souls, and this affects every area of our lives.

MALE LUST

Eldredge believes that the reason men fall into lust is because their manhood has been repressed, damaged, and managed. He says that it is "no coincidence" that men who are weary with daily tasks and responsibility have affairs for the "adventure" of it.[9] Wounded men, he believes, whose hearts have been "driven into the darker regions of the soul" are more likely to engage in pornography, deriving a "false strength" and sense of manliness from the activity.[10] Because he sees male sexual sin as "a battle for strength," Eldredge focuses on male freedom as the cure.[11]

According to Arterburn and Stoeker, God's call for sexual purity does not "come naturally" to men.[12] They believe that the male struggle with sexual lust is a result of their very "maleness."[13] Alongside this emphasis on men's susceptibility to lust, these authors teach that Christian manhood means the ability, given by God, to say no to sexual sin.[14] Harris believes that "purity does not happen by accident."[15] Whether a man lusts after a female friend, a woman he sees jogging, or a woman in a magazine, Arterburn and Stoeker believe that lust enslaves a man over a "series of bad decisions." They suggest practical ways to battle sexual sin in everyday life, such as understanding personal triggers, averting their eyes when they encounter certain women or images, and focusing on their wives as the object of their sexual desire.[16] And while there is certainly wisdom in this advice, I will address some of the troubling elements as well.

DISTRESSING DAMSELS

In purity rhetoric for men, women are often depicted as damsels in distress but also as damsels causing distress. It's confusing. Instead of encouraging men to heed Paul's advice to treat "older women as mothers, and younger women as sisters, with absolute purity" (1 Timothy 5:2), Christian books for men focus more on avoiding women than interacting with them. Sadly, there is little room for fellowship within the church between men and women when women are more often talked about as potential stumbling blocks than as sisters in Christ.

"A woman is at her best when she is being a woman," Eldredge says.[17] Being a woman, according to Eldredge, is about being "more seductive than fierce" and using one's beauty to "arouse" and captivate men.[18] Eldredge believes that the most important question for women is, "Am I lovely?"[19] He concludes that women would rather be valued for their beauty than their efficiency, independence, or service to others.[20] This view starkly contrasts the often referenced "Proverbs 31 woman," who is characterized by her mercy to the poor, her strength, and her desire to fear God over being charming or beautiful (Proverbs 31:20, 25, 30-31).

Eldredge quotes the poet William Blake who said, "The naked woman's body is a portion of eternity too great for the eye of man" and he holds up Ruth as an example of godly womanhood, summarizing the biblical story as one where Ruth seduces Boaz in order to secure his favor.[21]

> So what does Ruth do? She seduces him. . . . Ruth takes a bubble bath and puts on a knockout dress; then she waits for the right moment. . . . This is seduction pure and simple—and God holds it up for all women to follow when he not only gives Ruth her own book in the Bible but also names her in the genealogy. . . . I'm telling you

> that the church has really crippled women when it tells them that their beauty is vain and they are at their feminine best when they are "serving others." A woman is at her best when she is being a woman. Boaz needs a little help getting going and Ruth has some options. She can badger him: *all you do is work, work, work. Why won't you stand up and be a man?* She can whine about it: *Boaz, pleeease hurry up and marry me.* She can emasculate him: *I thought you were a real man; I guess I was wrong.* Or she can use all she is as a woman to get him to use all he's got as a man. She can arouse, inspire, energize. . . . Seduce him. Ask your man what he prefers.[22]

While Eldredge praises the beauty of women, purity rhetoric often depicts female beauty as a threat. Arterburn talks about the day he realized he was not honoring his wife, Sandy, in the way he looked at other women.[23] His solution was to avert or "bounce" his eyes away from women and images that inspired sexual lust.[24] While it is certainly wise to stop staring at someone you are lusting after, the rhetoric of avoidance begins to take on a dehumanizing tone. Instead of encouraging men to view women as sisters, Arterburn and Stoeker talk about how it is impossible to "eliminate attractive women," so they must instead "get zapped" by a man's metaphorical "clicker."[25] What they mean is that men should quickly avert their eyes when faced with visual temptation, but their language brings to mind the image of a buzzing, iridescent lantern that singes any bugs that fly too close. With so little advice offered to men about how to interact with women other than to avoid or "zap" them, women begin to resemble mosquitoes more than image bearers of God.

Although fighting sexual lust is biblical, depicting women as obstacles to and rewards for purity rather than as fellow image bearers of God is not. I asked Paul, a single Christian, his thoughts about how sexual purity is discussed in the church. He said,

> I don't think the idea that women are sexual objects was ever effectively refuted, since it was never replaced with an alternative approach to women. In fact, I think simply telling us not to lust almost affirmed the idea that women are sexual objects. But perhaps the biggest issue was not what was taught but simply that the topic was not discussed enough, not meaningfully anyway. Only in a token and shamed away.

"How will you talk to your son about lust in a way that affirms the dignity and value of women?" I asked him.

> I will tell my son that lust is deceitful. Lust tells you that sexual gratification is fulfilling, but there is no such thing as sexual gratification from an object. If you treat women like objects, you won't find satisfaction in that. Sexuality is about vulnerability and acceptance. You can only find those things in a person you respect. And respect doesn't mean treat politely and gentlemanly. Respect means that you think of the other person as being as much a person as you are.

Gardner remembers hearing a call for men to respect women at one of the Pure Freedom events she attended but notes that it seemed like a disconnected, "eleventh-hour" attempt in a day that focused almost entirely on male lust.[26] Harris stands out in his focus on women as "created in the image of God" and admits that he used to view women as "nothing more than objects to satisfy [his] desire," but when he gave up dating, he learned how to value women beyond their physical attractiveness and what they could do for him.[27] In general, though, the value of all women is not a main focus in purity teachings for men.

PROACTIVE VERSUS REACTIVE STRATEGIES

Books like *Every Man's Battle* reinforce lust as the problem, and rules like Graham's make avoiding women the solution. Christian writer Katelyn Beaty acknowledges that men who practice the Billy Graham rule likely do so with good motives, believing that "it's better to limit interacting with women altogether than open the door to temptation."[28] However, she also points out that this way of dealing with sexual sin elevates "personal purity" above the biblical command to love our neighbors.[29] Instead of teaching men to avoid women, a proactive strategy for battling sexual lust urges men to see women as neighbors.

Long-term solutions to the problem of sexual sin and abuse are not accomplished, as Hirsch points out, by "imposing distance between men and women."[30] Though there are times when a Christian must flee sexual temptation, like Joseph did from Potiphar's wife in Genesis 39, Christians must focus on proactive rather than reactive strategies. The problem of lust, as with any sin, must be discussed in light of the fact that Christians were created for community.

The apostle Peter calls Christians to "love one another earnestly from a pure heart" (1 Peter 1:22 ESV). If women are to be viewed as whole persons, the male gaze must be addressed holistically. The problem of male lust is not solved by looking away from women but by looking at them correctly—as more than their physical bodies, the temptations they pose, or the sexual satisfaction they provide. They must learn to see them as sisters, image bearers, and coheirs of the kingdom of God.

SEXUAL SELF-CONTROL AS POSSIBLE

In a recent episode of *The Unbreakable Kimmy Schmidt*, Kimmy explains that she is writing a children's book to help young boys learn how to treat girls because every boy has a monster living inside him. Some theologians might point out that the "monster" she refers to could be the sin nature.[31] I get that, but the idea that men straddle a line between monster and human is not biblical or helpful. It does not honor image bearers of God. Men and women have all sinned and fallen short of the glory of God (Romans 3:23), but our sin does not make us less human. Men are not monsters.

I think about what I would tell my son—that his body is a gift, something God declares good. That his sexuality is not a threat to fear or a weapon to wield. That women are not objects to use or to avoid but are beloved of God, partners in the gospel, and coheirs of the kingdom. That we are all image bearers of God but are born into Adam's sin. That we are endowed with dignity, but dignifying others is hard and takes care and effort. And that it is worth the effort, and God is with us as we wage war against sin and selfishness.

Klein observes that some men might worry "that they are monsters" while "others may feel their monstrous behavior is justified" because of the male reputation.[32] I wonder if both secular and Christian culture have contributed to a self-fulfilling prophecy. What is the long-term effect of telling our sons that their sexuality is a monster, which when unleashed is unstoppable? Does this help the cause of sexual purity?

Perhaps a better question to ask is, Is it true? Do men reach a point where they are physically unable to stop the sexual progression? Blake, a husband and father I interviewed, said: "The idea that once the drive starts, it can't stop—that's not true. It's hard. But it's not impossible. The Bible says one of the fruits of the Spirit is self-control. You can have that. God gives us [men] drives but he gives us brakes too." But purity culture tends to treat male lust as something that reaches a point where self-control is no longer an option. I would want to empower my own son with the truth that sexual self-control *is* possible.

We want our children to stay far away from temptation. That is wise. That is biblical. We see it all over the book of Proverbs. And we know, as adults, that the closer we get to temptation, the harder it is to say no. But Romans 8 makes it clear that those who are in Christ have been raised from the dead and given new life in Christ. The Holy Spirit dwells inside us. That is power—including power to say no to sexual sin.

When we talk to men about their lust more than their character, we fail them. When we focus on the physical appeal of women more than their value as image bearers, we are not helping the cause of purity. Daniel Darling suggests a "recovery of the robust Christian doctrine of human dignity."[33] This is essential when it comes to how we talk about men, women, and sexual purity in the church. We dehumanize women when we depict them as obstacles rather than allies in the faith, and we dehumanize men when we depict them as monsters who cannot control their lust. Instead, let self-control be taught not only as possible but as good for our flourishing within the church as beloved brothers and sisters in Christ. Let us begin with dignity and go from there.

DISCUSSION QUESTIONS

1. What do you think about the Billy Graham rule?
2. Did you read any of the books mentioned in this chapter? If so, how did they affect you?
3. How has biblical masculinity been depicted in your church? In what ways do you agree and/or disagree? Why are men often portrayed as "sex machines," and how does this image affect men and women, both in singleness and marriage?
4. Men, how were women depicted and discussed in male-only books, conferences, and conversations in your church? In what ways do you agree or disagree with these depictions?

5. Are there times to flee or avoid specific people? When and why?
6. In what ways should we talk *about* and *to* men differently?

ACTIVITY

As a group, create a list of stereotypes we have about men and a list of stereotypes we have about women. Take time to go through each one, trying to identify where these stereotypes originated (experience, secular culture, Christian culture, parents, books) and how we can combat them in order to view one another more wholly and as image bearers of God.

5

FIRST COMES LOVE, THEN COMES MARRIAGE

The church had a lot to say to me when I was in junior high and high school about sexual purity, but they have very little to say to me now that I'm in my thirties and still single.

Kristine Lavelle

I recently posed a question on Twitter to those who grew up in the church: What age did you think you'd be married by? I received 197 replies in less than twenty-four hours. My husband, who likes to pretend that he doesn't know what kind of book I'm writing—he pushes my buttons by telling people I'm writing a "sex book"—demonstrated that he really has been listening to my purity culture rants. When I pointed out the huge response to such a simple question, he said: "Maybe that's the pervasive, subtle influence of purity culture: that God has a timetable for a good Christian's life. Get married young or you will fall into sin."

"Get married young and have lots of babies," I added.

In purity culture, there are three main promises for those who practice abstinence: marriage, sex, and children. The thinking is that if teenagers are promised marriage by the time they graduate college, mind-blowing married sex, and a house full of adorable babies, then maybe, just maybe, they'll choose chastity. I will discuss problems with the promise of sex in the next chapter, but here I want to talk about three realities that these promises neglect: long-term singleness, infertility, and same-sex attraction. Ignoring these realities alienates those who struggle with them and pushes them to the margins of our churches.

Tables have become a popular analogy for inclusion. Christians are encouraged to make sure their metaphorical table is long enough and wide enough to welcome anyone to the conversation. It makes me think about Thanksgiving dinners and how there was always a table for the adults and a smaller table—in the corner or all the way in the kitchen—for the kids. If we ran out of space around the adult table, we had to decide who to move to the kid's table.

The promises in purity culture include the majority who get married and have children. But they alienate those who don't fit into the heteronormative, nuclear family, making them the easy pick for the kid's table, with knees pushed up to their chests, straining to hear the conversation happening in the other room.

THE NEGLECTED REALITY OF SINGLENESS

My goal on Sunday mornings is simple: hug as many widows as I can. Maybe eighty-year-old women are not the first who come to mind when we think about singles in the church, but they are those for whom there are no college Bible studies or singles mixers. They are two who have become one, with boxes unopened in the attic and grandchildren busy with after-school sports, trying to figure out how to sleep alone after decades beside the warmth of another person. I hug them because I remember how it felt to not have my husband beside me.

It felt like starving. All I could think about some days was how much I missed the instant comfort of his arms encircling me. I was married less than five years, but I had grown used to the therapy of daily hugs. When he divorced me, it was the thing I missed most. So much some days that I would look down at my chest to see if there was any physical evidence of the ache I felt inside. Hollow. Empty. Like part of me was withering away.

And I wonder if Jesus ever looked down at his own chest as it tightened from the grief of John the Baptist's death, or the ache of homesickness for heaven, and wondered why God didn't give him a wife to embrace. Singleness is not a curse or a problem to fix—but it can be so lonely. And, as my wise friend Jillian has pointed out, loneliness *is* a form of suffering. This is just one thing we will learn when we draw near to the singles in our midst.

Perhaps we will also learn about art, or theology, or web design. For instance, my friend Holly Stallcup is creating a house for women where they can study the Bible, rest, create, and learn from one another, free of cost. My brother, Joel, is single and has been immersed in the culinary world the last few years and is now the head chef at a Japanese restaurant. I love seeing his passion and learning about what he does—most recently, about the art of filleting a fish. My friend Michaela serves at a local camp, where she gets to invest in the lives of teenagers, providing a listening ear and words of life.

We are more than our relationship status. Singles are artists. Chefs. Theologians. They get lonely. They get excited. They are worth seeking out, investing in, and listening to. Sadly, one woman I interviewed, Janna, shared that it wasn't until she started dating her husband that she suddenly felt visible to others in her church. Those who are part of a couple, and even more so those who are married with children, seem to be at the center of our churches. They tend to be the majority. Our desire for singles to "graduate" and join the marrieds is not always selfless. Sure, we want them to experience our joy, but if we are honest with ourselves, we also want the convenience of sameness.

The way we regularly ignore Paul's advice to the Corinthians says something about how we view singleness in the church. We don't value it. We create space for it only as a season, not as a legitimate, lifelong calling. And we hold the nuclear family up so high, it is at risk of falling off its pedestal. And maybe it should. We need to ask ourselves why the church views singleness as a problem to solve.

Sam Allberry suggests that it is celibacy which causes our true discomfort. Deep down, many of us believe that "without sex you can't really experience what it means to be truly human."[1] Singles, therefore, are incomplete—less human—until they find their match. In contrast, the apostle Paul says that singleness is actually better. It frees individuals up to focus more on the things of God. Paul does not vilify marriage—he cannot do so when marriage was God's idea—but he seems to view it as more distracting than singleness:

> I would like you to be free from concern. An unmarried man is concerned about the Lord's affairs—how he can please the Lord. But a married man is concerned about the affairs of this world—how he can please his wife—and his interests are divided. An unmarried woman or virgin is concerned about the Lord's affairs: Her aim is to be devoted to the Lord in both body and spirit. But a married woman is concerned about the affairs of this world—how she can please her husband. I am saying this for your own good, not to restrict you, but that you may live in a right way in undivided devotion to the Lord. (1 Corinthians 7:32-35)

But we flip this around. We view singleness as the distraction and marriage as the ideal. And, honestly, in our sex-obsessed, family-worshiping culture and churches, singleness probably *is* more distracting. Instead of encouraging singles to live with gusto in the circumstance they are in, we push them to change that circumstance. I catch myself asking my husband, "Who can we set her up with?" Or I think, "It would be awkward for him to join, when everyone else is married," as I plan our next Bible study. And in these small comments and passing thoughts, I contribute to a church culture that marginalizes singles.

Less than two years ago, I was single. And it was one thing to be unattached in my twenties, when the longing for companionship was easily satisfied, being surrounded by others in the same circumstance. We were all single then, eager to find our life callings, to serve, and take road trips. There was loneliness and disappointment, but singleness did not feel as strange when I was young. By twenty-four, I was married. But at twenty-nine, I was single again—and it was different this time.

Being single in my thirties was lonelier. I had more confidence and direction, so I plunged right into graduate school, leading Bible studies, and writing the books I had always wanted to write. But when I looked around, there were so few of us. Getting coffee with someone required a string of text messages and the double-checking of appointment books. Even then, most people chose to spend their limited free time with their families. People were kind and loving to me in my singleness, but I knew I stood out.

Not all singles desire marriage. But for those who do, the advice to "find someone to settle down with" or "focus on your love life" is not helpful. In fact, it often presses a wound. One woman I interviewed, Erica, admitted her frustration that "some of us do burn but can't marry." While even Paul tells those who desire marriage to go ahead and get married, the reality is, marriage is not always an option. Despite prayers and multiple dating apps, many singles who desire marriage remain single.

Instead of pursuing her dreams during singleness, Erica felt like she was "basically treading water," waiting for marriage. With all the rhetoric about waiting in purity culture, it's easy to view singleness as something to survive rather than a time to flourish. "I've found a way to true, deep peace with my single life," Erica said, "but it took a lot of years and heartache to get there." She continued: "I wish someone had guided me in my late teens and early twenties with more than platitudes about how I should 'wait and prepare' (as though my whole life didn't count and was just preparation for marriage) or empty promises that 'God is going to write you a wonderful love story' (which isn't much help when you don't know when or if the love story will ever come)."

We can make space for singles at the dining room table by valuing them where they are at, not where they might end up. We can hire single pastors. We can ask singles to lead Bible studies and join our leadership teams. We can invite them into our homes. Jesus himself was single: Would we relegate him to the kids' table, forcing him to sit on a too small plastic chair? Singles do not belong at the margins of our churches. No one does.

And we need to crush the myth that good sexual behavior is rewarded with marriage. The longer we teach this—the longer we talk about marriage as a God-given promise or a Christian's highest good—the more we set singles up to feel abandoned by God. A young woman recently described to me how it feels to be promised marriage and remain single:

> I am so angry at God because I feel bait-and-switched. I was raised to value marriage, to prepare myself for a life with a spouse and children. I did everything right. I kept myself sexually pure, I prayed for my future husband every night, I learned the skills I was supposed to learn, I was obedient to my parents when they told me not to

> act on crushes or date around. I did everything I was supposed to and the life I planned for, the life I was told that God was preparing me for, isn't showing up, and it doesn't look like it is going to any time soon. I asked for bread, and I am chewing on gravel.

We create opportunities to be disappointed with God when we put our hope in things he never promised. Jesus did not die so that Christians could live out their own Nicholas Sparks novel. He died to set us free from slavery to sin, to make us new, and to draw us into the kingdom of God forever. It is not earthly marriage but the marriage supper of the Lamb that we are promised. It is adoption as sons and daughters that we receive, not because we stayed sexually pure or dressed modestly but because Jesus spilled his blood for our sins. Whatever our relationship status on earth, Christians can stand firm in their identity as children of the living God and as the church, his body, and his bride.

THE NEGLECTED REALITY OF INFERTILITY

"It didn't even cross my mind," Jaclyn told me. "I thought, 'Of course I'll have children.' But the reality is, that didn't happen." I've known Jaclyn most of my life. She and her husband are two of the kindest people you will ever meet—the type you can pray with or watch *Seinfeld* with—whichever you need. She makes the best apple pie and he loves to lead worship at church. They are funny and warm, and they would be amazing parents. But instead, they have walked a long road of infertility, with surprises, surgeries, and loss—so much loss. Jaclyn's tears have been my tears, and I have prayed often that God would give them a child.

"We are still met with a lot of surprise when people find out we can't have kids," she told me.

"But there are *so* many Bible stories about infertility!" I said, incredulous.

"I know," she said. We talked about the characters in Scripture who dealt with this pain. Abraham and Sarah. Rachel and Jacob. "Hannah was wailing," she said. "I think that is a picture of the inner turmoil. That's what it feels like. It's agonizing. Infertility affects one in eight couples, and I just feel like there is a lack of discussion in the church about it. People don't know what to do with us."

In one of the more popular books of the modern purity culture era, *And the Bride Wore White*, Dannah Gresh says that God loves to bless our sexual obedience by giving us children: "*If* you will wait, *then* you'll make babies with great celebration."[2] I have no wish to demonize Gresh, who is a wonderful woman of God. In fact, I have a hunch that in hindsight she might not repeat this promise today. Her goal here was to encourage young women to save sex for marriage. This is biblical. She also wanted them to understand that having children inside the marriage covenant is God's design for procreation rather than engaging in premarital sex and risking teen pregnancy. This promise also relates to her warnings about STDs and the genuine physical harm they can cause, including infertility.

But the idea that disobedience always leads to negative consequences and that obedience always leads to tangible blessings, like babies, is not true. It is rather one of the many ways the prosperity gospel shows up in purity culture. Look around. Are the chaste the ones now married, having amazing sex all the time? Do the most nurturing men and women in your church have a bushel of children playing at their feet? We read about blessings and consequences in books like Proverbs, but these are principles, not guarantees.

Those who wait to have sex until marriage are not promised children. Neither are the sexually immoral cursed with barrenness. I am a believer in the sovereignty of God, but who he decides to bless with children and when is a true mystery to me. Too often, it is discomfort with this mystery that leads us to blanket statements like, "It will happen for you one day" and "Just trust God and he will grant you the desire of your heart."

Fertility is affected by many factors. Cancer treatments can cause infertility. Autoimmune diseases, such as endometriosis, can make getting pregnant difficult or even impossible. So can hormone imbalances or low sperm count. And sometimes couples never get a clear answer as to why they can't conceive. We live on the other side of the fall, and our bodies bear its weight. But in our grief over infertility and our longing for all things to be made new, we have a Savior who is well acquainted with grief and a God who hears our every cry.

God understands. But does the church? Despite Scripture's acknowledgement of infertility—Sarah's waiting and Hannah's weeping—it is a form of suffering that too often goes unaddressed. Maura A. Ryan says that she can't remember a time when the "pain of *longing for* parenthood was acknowledged liturgically alongside the joy and struggles of its realization."[3] Instead, infertility is often downplayed as a desire that could be "easily redirected toward adoption."[4] The mere act of acknowledging infertility as suffering could help restore the faith of those walking through it.

But we panic at other people's pain, especially when we don't understand it. Theologian Stanley Hauerwas talks about attempting to console a friend whose mother had committed suicide. He admits, "I did not want to go because I knew there was nothing I could do or say to make things even appear better than they were."[5] Despite feeling ill-equipped, he discovered he had the ability to "be present."[6] We do not know the plans of God, but we can sit with one another in our confusion and unmet longings. Together we can cling to the promise that God is good.

I talked to my friend Aarik Danielsen about his and his wife's experience. They have both struggled with infertility.

Aarik grew up in the church, and while no one ever specifically told him, "You will have children if you obey God," all he ever saw were young Christians getting married and starting their families. He told me that it has been shame more than guilt that he and his wife have struggled with. "Why us?" he has often wondered, looking at the ease with which other couples get pregnant. I asked him how the church could better love those struggling with infertility. "Just acknowledging us and saying, 'Hey, we see you.'" He added that when others get pregnant, "I never ever want to mute someone's joy. I'm really happy for them, but I also grieve. It's both."

I remember the hard but necessary conversation I had with my friend about this. I asked her, "If I ever get pregnant, how do you want me to tell you?"

She paused for a while before answering. "I don't want you to hold anything back," she said, "You're my friend and I love you. I will be so happy for you. But I also might need a second."

"That makes sense," I told her. And we sat in silence on a park bench, holding our coffee, with fall leaves blowing around our feet. So much of love consists of conversations like this, where we admit we don't know what to do or say. I'm thankful for my friend's patience with me, and her honesty.

Aarik told me that loving the infertile is more about sitting with them in their grief than giving them false assurance or empty encouragement. And I believe that we must show those struggling with infertility that they are seen in the church and have value *now*, even if they never have children. What would it look like if our sermons and liturgies included the kind of hope the childless need to keep the faith, if we took time to "make the invisible struggle of the infertile visible?"[7] I picture a Mother's Day Sunday where not only those with children but those who have lost children or who are unable to conceive are acknowledged, maybe even in the form of a song or prayer of lament. There is a place for rejoicing with those who rejoice but also for weeping with those who weep.

Maybe one reason we fail to weep with the infertile is because we are too busy giving them advice. As Jesus was walking with his disciples one day, he saw a blind man. The man had been blind since the day he was born. His disciples immediately flew to judgment. "Rabbi," they asked, "who sinned, this man or his parents, that he was born blind?" (John 9:2). Jesus was quick to correct them, pointing out that the man's blindness had nothing to do with generational sin or punishment. "Neither this man nor his parents sinned," Jesus said, "but this happened so that the works of God might be displayed in him" (John 9:3).

Despite our theology, we often assume that a person's suffering is the result of their sin. Or if not their sin, a lack of effort, or ignorance, or some other personal failing. Instead of empathy, we approach the hurting with suggestions and recommendations. I asked those struggling with infertility to share some of the unsolicited advice they have received over the years from fellow Christians. They've been told: "Just relax." "Find a better doctor." "Try this essential oil." "Try this sex position."

Coralie Cowan writes about sitting under Pastor John MacArthur's preaching on Mother's Day in 1987. She says that he preached the following: "That's why the goal of becoming a godly mother is the highest and most noble pursuit of womanhood. God has specially equipped women for that very purpose, and in Christ, women can experience profound satisfaction in that divinely ordained pursuit. They can be who God created them to be."

Hearing these words, she wept, thinking: "If it is the highest, and noblest pursuit of womanhood, I must assume, that no matter how I strive to seek after God and walk by faith and be filled by the Spirit and study to show myself approved, I will only ever be second best, unless God opens my womb."[8]

Another woman, Brittany, said that people assumed God must be teaching her a lesson—either that she needed to be more content, less anxious, or stop making an idol out of parenthood. Once she fixed those things, God would give her children. Others shared that they were told that their infertility was God's way of telling them to adopt or foster—putting pressure on them to grow their family in a specific way, whether they felt called to it or not.

I heard over and over again how couples were told that once they adopted, they would get pregnant because it had happened to so-and-so. Other comments included: "You waited too long to get married." "You shouldn't have put your career first."

Megan, who is single, shared with me that people talk about her future children as a fact, when she knows that she is physically unable to conceive. This pains her. Another woman shared that after she miscarried and lost both her grandparents in the same year, friends assured her that her next pregnancy would survive because "God wouldn't cause that much pain all at once." A week later, she found out she had miscarried again. And one woman's three-word response to my question about how people have responded to her infertility hit me in the gut: "Lack of faith." It brought me back to the blind man Jesus healed. Who sinned that this man was born blind? Who sinned that this woman is unable to conceive?

It seems we are so uncomfortable with the reality of suffering that our theology has stopped short. Instead of looking to God's Word, which is full of sinner-saints suffering persecution, loss, and infertility, we fumble to explain what God has not answered. We deny the truth of pain. We gloss over what deserves to be mourned, and we cannot comfortably sit in silence with the hurting. This must change.

THE NEGLECTED REALITY OF SAME-SEX ATTRACTION

I noticed something as I reread the books from my youth on dating, purity, and preparing for marriage. My friend was missing. And my other friend. More than just them, an entire group of people was ignored. I looked for them, skimming the pages to catch a glimpse, but there was no mention of them anywhere.

Same-sex attracted (SSA) Christians have no place in purity culture. It is not that they are demonized—they aren't even acknowledged. Every bit of advice is geared toward cisgender heterosexuals, which leaves out other orientations as well. While I will focus on the same-sex attracted, how purity culture rhetoric ignored and affected those who identify as asexual, nonbinary, or bisexual, for example, is also a conversation worth having.

I wonder if SSA teens felt like ghosts at True Love Waits rallies, or like mutants in youth group. If your struggle is not even acknowledged out loud, what does that do to your sense of self? Your sense of community? Your faith?

I can only imagine the isolation they experienced when the only carrot dangled as motivation for pursuing sexual abstinence was the promise of heterosexual marriage, sex, and family. Surely, the only hope a same-sex attracted Christian could cling to after hearing such a promise was that God might change their attraction.

In her book *Gay Girl, Good God,* Jackie Hill Perry admits: "I was attracted to women before I knew how to spell my name."[9] She was surprised when her attractions didn't immediately change after she gave her life to Christ. Soon after her conversion, she found herself noticing a pretty customer in line at the store where she worked, wondering if she could get her attention. But instead of proceeding, she writes that a "quiet war" began inside of her. Conviction. The power of the Holy

Spirit. "Wanting God over a woman was an entirely new experience for me."[10]

Perry says that it is a lie that all same-sex desires magically transform into heterosexual ones at the moment of salvation.[11] What changed for her was a desire for God. It changed everything, including her ability to comfortably return to old habits and thought patterns. She could no longer pursue the life she had lived before her conversion. She was a new creation.

Gardner asks the revealing question: "Does the argument for abstinence crumble if the goal of abstinence—marriage—is unattainable?"[12] The answer is yes. If we tell Christians to hold on to sexual purity *until* they get married, we are failing both straight and same-sex attracted Christians. We are telling them that there is a finish line to purity this side of heaven; a day when their sexual longings will finally be fulfilled. Not only is this idea unbiblical, it leaves our SSA brothers and sisters looking off into the distance for a goal post that doesn't exist. It sets them up for defeat. If the only reason to pursue purity is a relationship they won't ever achieve, why pursue it at all?

Our purity rhetoric needs to change if we want to honor Scripture and create an atmosphere of community, guidance, and love for those wrestling with same-sex attraction. To do this, we must revisit the goal of sexual purity. Or rather, what the goal is *not*. Marriage is not the goal of purity. Family is not the goal. Sex is not the goal. God and his glory are the goal of purity. Practicing purity is a form of worship, another way we get to praise God through obedience with our bodies, hearts, and thoughts. It's another way to thank him for rescuing us from the domain of darkness and transferring us into the kingdom of his beloved Son. We are called to purity because we are called to be like Jesus, our Creator, God, and friend, who is *holy, holy, holy*. Pursuing purity is not a transaction. It is worship.

I have learned more from my same-sex attracted brothers and sisters about what it means to live fully for God than I have from anyone else. If you do not know, read, or listen to SSA Christians, you are missing out. Among them are Henri Nouwen, Wesley Hill, Rosaria Butterfield, Sam Allberry, Jackie Hill Perry, and Rachel Gilson. Some have gone on to enter straight marriages, while others continue to pursue celibacy in singleness. I watch their lives and learn so much from the way they make Jesus their ultimate source of satisfaction. I am beyond grateful for these siblings in Christ and their dedication to sexual purity at the highest cost.

I want to speak to one friend in particular. You know who you are. And when you read this, I want you to know that you are beloved. You are a treasure to God and to me. To all of us. Your sins are no more heinous than my own. God's mercy is no less consuming, no less extravagant for you than it is for me. The way you submit to God every day, even when you feel alone and weary from the fight, encourages my faith. And one day we will be in heaven together, if not sitting on a cloud, then as light as a cloud. No more guilt. No more shame. No more secrets. You will not carry this burden forever. But while you do, know that you are not alone.

Pearcey notes that Jesus is the role model for all singles, having lived "a fully human life without sex, romance, or marriage."[13] If we never marry, we will still know what it is like to be loved fully and known intimately—by God himself. Just as Jesus' singleness did not keep him from friendship, our singleness should not be practiced apart from the gift of community and our family, the church. But as we acknowledge those with same-sex attraction in our churches, we must recognize that many are living in silence and fear. They worry about what will happen if they share their particular brand of temptation. While temptations toward gossip or pride might be easy to discuss with other people, sexual temptation is still often taboo and kept quiet, especially same-sex attraction.

I asked a friend of mine to share with me a few reasons she finds it challenging to talk about her same-sex attraction with other Christians:

- She worries that, in sharing, she will gain a permanent label based on her attractions.
- People she has told in the past have assumed that she must have been sexually abused as a child. (She was not.)
- Some have been quick to dismiss her attraction as a fad or "not really a sexual attraction."
- She worries that other women will feel uncomfortable around her, mistaking her genuine affection and desire for same-sex friendship as sexual attraction or lust.
- She knows that some people will be shocked, assuming that a feminine pastor's daughter, saved at a young age, would never find herself sexually attracted to women.

And, I will add one more reason, based on what I have heard Christians say about the same-sex attracted. Some people assume that a Christian experiencing same-sex attraction must be fanning the flame somehow, whether through pornography, fantasizing, or sex. They cannot imagine a faithful Christian continuing to struggle with same-sex attraction.

But the most common reason I have heard from same-sex attracted Christians as to why they are hesitant to share their struggle is shame. When Wesley Hill spoke at the Revoice conference in 2018, he invited his audience to remember a time when they felt this shame. "Maybe," he said, "it was when you heard a denunciation from the pulpit, the likes of which you'd never heard about any other sin, and you internalized the thought that somehow [you] must be worse, [you] must be more broken, [you] must be more fundamentally askew than anyone else sitting in this church, and you felt the weight of shame bearing down on you."[14]

He went on to talk about the woman caught in adultery, noting how Jesus was not interested in "rewriting the rulebook" or "undermining God's holy will for our lives." Rather, Jesus sought to remind those around her, who held stones in their hands ready to hurl them at her, that they were also sinners and that they needed grace too. Hill acknowledges that, as a celibate gay Christian, it can be hard to submit to God's sexual ethic. "We may struggle with it—I struggle with it," he said, but "we don't want to adjust or trim down the law of God to fit our own proclivities."

Hill encourages his audience that, regardless of their sexual attraction, each of us is in "profound solidarity with one another, not only in condemnation but in redemption." We are on equal ground before God, both as sinners and, in Christ, as beloved children. "We have been set free to say no to sexual sin and yes to friendship, yes to community, yes to hospitality, yes to service, yes to beauty," Hill says. "We are liberated because of Christ."

Many will look at this liberty and shake their heads, arguing that true spiritual freedom includes the right to sexual expression, whether one is straight, same-sex attracted, or bisexual. Maybe you are that person. This issue is "dividing even conservative religious groups," as Nancy Pearcey points out, referencing a 2014 survey that found that "51 percent of evangelical millennials said same-sex behavior is morally acceptable."[15]

Nadia Bolz-Weber tells the story of a woman named Cindy, who decided to deal with her same-sex attraction by tearing out every passage from her Bible that mentioned homosexuality and burning it: "As she stood there watching the inferno, she felt as if the people of her childhood church, the youth workers and pastors and other adults, rose from the grave of her psyche and stood in judgement of her around that fire. She saw them, but she didn't care. She was allowing herself to be free."[16]

Beloved, this is not freedom. Sin distracts us with lies about agency and choice while binding our hands and feet. It tells us that unbridled sexual expression is the definition of freedom, when in fact, sin is a slave-driver. It tempts and lures, then places a yoke around our necks.

> Therefore, brothers and sisters, we have an obligation—but it is not to the flesh, to live according to it. For if you live according to the flesh, you will die; but if by the Spirit you put to death the misdeeds of the body, you will live. For those who are led by the Spirit of God are the children of God. The Spirit you received does not make you slaves, so that you live in fear again; rather, the Spirit you received brought about your adoption to sonship. And by him we cry, *"Abba,* Father." The Spirit himself testifies with our spirit that we are God's children. Now if we are children, then we are heirs—heirs of God and co-heirs with Christ, if indeed we share in his sufferings in order that we may also share in his glory. (Romans 8:12-17)

We know you, God. You did not discover sex and then create rules around it. You invented sex for marriage and for your glory. The Garden of Eden, before Adam and Eve sinned, is our model. But we live in a post-Fall reality, God, and it's hard. It's wearying to say no to things our bodies crave. It is lonely to watch others go on to date and marry while we live alone. Sometimes it seems like obeying you means starvation, cruel punishment that harms not only our bodies but our emotions and the dreams we had for our lives. Sometimes, God, we just want to give up.

Let us not confuse the broad road for the long table. There is space down the narrow path Jesus walked for a table filled with as many ragamuffins as would come and dine. Don't worry about your clothes. You don't need to bring a side dish.

Sit your weary bones down. I will keep a seat open beside me, if you don't mind sitting next to someone who fails often, someone who gets so caught up in herself that she might forget to pass you the salt.

You are not alone in your struggle against the flesh. Your temptations do not exclude you from God's grace, and neither does it dampen his love for you or your value in the church. Your same-sex attraction does not put a chip in your dignity as a precious image bearer of God. Bolz-Weber is right when she points out that the same-sex attracted among us are too often pushed to the margins of our churches. They are. And we need to fix that. But the solution is not to preach a false freedom. Rather, let us welcome one another into the gathering of sinner-saints, reminding each other of the hope of Christ and the comfort of communion with his body.

Father, help us to love one another with empathy and wisdom as we stand on the truth of your Word, bursting with hope.

LIVING WITH LONGING

After my divorce, I started making plans to buy a tiny house. You know, the ones where the microwave is stacked on top of the washing machine under the kitchen sink, which doubles as a dining room table? I pictured myself living on someone's acreage and maybe setting up an overhang outside the front door, where I could sit in the cool of the morning with a cup of coffee. I was lonely, broken, and trustless, unready to try marriage again. But God had different plans.

I met a widower—on Twitter, of all places. A pastor who lived in Iowa with his old dog, Frank. We tweeted, emailed, and wrote each other handwritten letters that turned into love notes. He proposed to me on a mountain, we got married in my father's church, and honestly I have never been happier. But new love does not erase old wounds. It helps—Evan has been such a healing presence in my life, from his stability and his faithfulness to his hugs—but both of us live with loss every day. My life cannot erase his first wife's death. His faithfulness cannot erase the pain of my divorce. Good things don't make bad things disappear. They coexist.

My husband and I are content, but we both live with longing. We are married, we get to have sex (yay!) and maybe children (we'll see), but none of that changes the fact that we have stared death and rejection in the face, and we will never be the same. We will always long for a world that is not broken. I may have what you want. You may have what I want. But changing circumstances cannot fix the longing we were born with—a longing that only Jesus' return can satisfy.

Our earthly longings are real. We long for intimacy. Someone to fall asleep laughing with. Someone to kiss without restraint. We long to hold a child in our arms and call it our own. We long for family. We long to be loved with commitment and fidelity. We long for a home that is filled with conversation and joy, rather than the echoes of Netflix continuous play. Molly Jasinski beautifully writes about her desire for marriage: "The only thing I do know, the only thing in this life I am truly sure of, is that God is good. Whether this longing is ever fulfilled or not."[17]

For those on the verge of giving up in order to satisfy these longings—hold on. Not for marriage or sex or children, but for God and his glory. Your faith is not in vain. Your self-control is not for nothing. Your trust in Jesus is well-placed. Consider Jesus. Consider the glory that is to be revealed. Consider that you were bought with a price. Whether you are married, single, same-sex attracted, lonely, infertile, transgender, divorced, asexual, whoever you are—you matter. Your longings matter. And submitting them to God's holy, precious will matters.

Lauren Winner talks about chastity as a way of keeping vigil. She compares the life of chastity to the monks and ascetics who would fast from food and sleep to remind themselves of their hunger for God. She says that keeping vigil through chastity is not about rejecting something just to reject it but about actively pursuing union with Jesus and the church.[18] I love this way of thinking about sexual purity because I believe it is what Paul meant when he talked about singleness as an undistracted life of devotion to Christ. Karen Swallow Prior writes about childlessness in a similar way, concluding that, despite her desire to be a mom, God has given her opportunities unique to someone without children, to serve the church and be a light for the gospel. She concludes: "We know that in heaven there will be no more marriage or giving in marriage; our earthly unions are but temporal signposts of the eternal union of Christ and his bride. . . . If, for now, we are poor or broken, childless or spouseless, waiting or wanting—yet obedient—we are not failures. We are called his children."[19]

Paul tells the Philippian church "the Lord is near, do not be anxious about anything" (Philippians 4:5-6). Do you long for companionship, but aren't attracted to the opposite gender? Do not be anxious, beloved. Your commitment to obedience is a light. Your surrender to God is not in vain. The Lord is near. The church is strengthened by your faith. Do you desire marriage, but are continually discouraged by the dating scene, the singles at church, and the emphasis on romantic love everywhere you look? Do not be anxious, beloved. You will not miss out on true love. Sex isn't it. Marriage isn't it. Jesus is returning soon, in all his glory.

Those of us who are in Christ are already a part of a family, whether we ever get married or have children. We are the body of Christ, the family of God. And this is the family that continues on into eternity. There is no sex in heaven, no marriage, no giving birth. These earthly gifts are beautiful, God-created glimpses of his love, but they are soon passing away. The apostle James calls our lives a vapor. Marriage is a vapor.

Children are a vapor. But our union with Christ and with one another lasts into eternity.

> Because we know that the one who raised the Lord Jesus from the dead will also raise us with Jesus and present us with you to himself.
>
> Therefore we do not lose heart. Though outwardly we are wasting away, yet inwardly we are being renewed day by day. For our light and momentary troubles are achieving for us an eternal glory that far outweighs them all. So we fix our eyes not on what is seen, but on what is unseen, since what is seen is temporary, but what is unseen is eternal. (2 Corinthians 4:14, 16-18)

As Jackie Hill Perry says, we are not called to a "heterosexual gospel," where marriage is the thing that makes us finally whole. Marriage is not the goal of obedience. She says that "the reason to turn from sin has *always* been so we can turn toward Jesus."[20] And Jesus does not offer us a sugary drink that temporarily slakes our thirst. He offers us living water, a gospel drink that wells up to eternal life.

Here on earth, we will struggle with loneliness. Some of us will struggle with childlessness. With unrequited love. With impossible love. We will face desires we cannot satisfy, longings that will cause our hearts and bodies to ache, and sometimes we will wonder if carrying this cross of Christ is worth it. We will wonder if he really does understand. When you feel that God cannot possibly understand what you are going through, consider the "days of his flesh" (Hebrews 5:7 RSV). He can. He does. Jesus too has a body.

DISCUSSION QUESTIONS

1. What age did you think you'd be married by?
2. If you grew up in the church, what were you taught about singleness? What do you believe about it now? If you are

single, what do you wish other people in the church understood about singleness?

3. How can we do a better job of loving, valuing, and reaching out to the singles in our churches? List at least three practical steps.
4. If you grew up in the church, what were you taught about family and procreation? What do you believe now?
5. If you have personally struggled with infertility and are willing to share, how have you been treated by other Christians, and what do you wish they understood about infertility?
6. How can we do a better job of loving, valuing, and reaching out to the childless in our churches? Think of at least three practical ways.
7. How does your church talk about same-sex attraction? In what ways do you agree or disagree? If you are same-sex attracted and willing to share: How have you been treated by others in the church and what do you wish they understood?
8. How can we do a better job of loving, valuing, and reaching out to the same-sex attracted in our churches?
9. What are some practical and God-honoring ways we can respond to unmet longings?

ACTIVITY

Divide into groups of two or three and take turns sharing at least one unmet longing you are dealing with right now. Pray for one another about these longings.

6

PROBLEMS WITH THE PROMISE OF SEX

The problem is not that we talk about sex.
The problem is how we talk about sex.

LAUREN WINNER

How do you convince a room full of teenagers to chant "sex is great" while simultaneously signing abstinence pledge cards? According to Christine Joy Gardner, by making chastity sexy. Gardner attended numerous purity events hosted by groups such as Pure Freedom, Silver Ring Thing, and True Love Waits, and conducted over sixty interviews with the leaders and attendees. She notes how modern evangelical purity culture borrowed strategies from pop culture to make the message of abstinence more winsome. She writes, "Silver Ring Thing events have been described as part rave, part *Saturday Night Live,* and part Saturday night revival."[1]

The promise of sex in marriage was the carrot dangled in front of teenagers to get them to commit to abstinence. And while this sexy carrot may have convinced youth to chant, clap, and sign pledge cards, it ultimately made sex less about the union between two self-giving, embodied souls in marriage and more about a future reward for sexual restraint.

And it made promises it couldn't keep. Sara Moslener, author of *Virgin Nation*, says that early purity reformers taught that men who practiced sexual self-control were "promised health, happiness, and a wholesome (i.e., married) life."[2] The modern purity movement made similar promises, accompanied by strobe lights and the music of Usher. One young man admitted to Gardner that he had committed to sexual abstinence in order to give himself the gift of "future happiness in marriage." Purity advocates hoped that the promise of healthy, satisfying marriages would "curb sexual temptation" in adolescents. However, Gardner points out that this goal changed the motivation for sexual abstinence from "pleasing God to pleasing oneself."[3]

SEX AS A REWARD

Like many young stars, Justin Bieber got caught up in immorality and partying. But more recently, Bieber has been attending Hillsong Church in New York City. Not only that, but he decided to practice celibacy with his fiancée, Hailey, before their wedding day. He talked about his decision with *Vogue* magazine, explaining:

> [God] doesn't ask us not to have sex for him because he wants rules and stuff. . . . He's like, I'm trying to protect you from hurt and pain. I think sex can cause a lot of pain. Sometimes people have sex because they don't feel good enough. Because they lack self-worth. Women do that, and guys do that. I wanted to rededicate myself to God in that way because I really felt it was better for the condition of my soul. And I believe that God blessed me with Hailey as a result. There are perks. You get rewarded for good behavior.[4]

I appreciate Bieber's commitment to chastity before marriage, but I am concerned with his motivation. I don't blame him—this is what we have been teaching for years. But what happens when adolescents are taught that good sexual behavior is always rewarded with timely marriage and amazing sex, and these promises fail to materialize or live up to the hype? They might wonder what else the church is lying about.

In purity rhetoric, married sex is the prize. Rebecca St. James imagines, with a romantic flourish, the honeymoon of a couple who waited for marriage to have sex, while Gresh recounts her own wedding night, sharing how it surpassed her and her husband's expectations.[5] Over and over again in the books of my youth, the promise was repeated that saving sex for marriage is "worth the wait."[6] In *I Kissed Dating Goodbye,* Harris says that a commitment to sexual purity in singleness is like "delaying our gratification" and "storing up passion" that will make married sex more meaningful.[7] And Arterburn and Stoeker talk in *Every Man's Battle* about the "physically gratifying pay off that comes from obedience to God's sexual standards."[8]

One woman, Marta, told me she was taught that if she saved sex for marriage, she would "have an amazing sex life with no problems at all." Sarah added that marriage between two virgins was portrayed as "mind-blowing" and "effortlessly fantastic." By emphasizing the joy and pleasure of sex in marriage, purity culture was able to rightly assure young men and women that there *is* a God-honoring context for sex. It also challenged religious arguments about procreation being the only purpose for sex in marriage. I praise God for this. But somewhere along the line modern purity culture turned married sex from a blessing into a trophy. And God never treats sex this way.

Sex is not a reward for good behavior. If it were, all the godly, chaste men and women we know would be married right now, having fantastic sex and making lots of beautiful babies without any struggles with illness or infertility. If sex is something you earn by pure behavior, then our friends who sleep with their boyfriends and girlfriends outside of marriage would all be impotent or having terrible sex. Obviously this is not the case.

The reality is that one of my closest friends has been faithful to God's sexual ethic her entire life. She spends her time teaching at-risk children how to read. She is a foster parent. She babysits for her married friends on the weekends so they can have date nights. She paints beautifully and sings while she cooks. She loves her local church and studies the Scriptures diligently. She is beautiful, warm, and kind—and she is still unmarried.

The reality is that my husband and his first wife didn't kiss until the altar. A year into their marriage, she got cancer and eventually got so sick that she couldn't have sex. Before she died, she was told that the chemotherapy had made her infertile, dashing her dream of ever having children. They were obedient to God's Word, pure and faithful, and they still suffered immensely in their marriage.

The reality is that I saved myself for my first husband. He was my first kiss, and I was a virgin on our wedding night. Then, almost five years into our marriage, he left the Christian faith and divorced me. I remember physically aching from the lack of touch and the bruise of abandonment. What do you do when you follow all the rules and find yourself divorced at age twenty-nine, childless, no longer a virgin, with a heavy load of trust issues slung over your shoulder?

The reality is that, despite being warned about guilt, STDs, and teen pregnancy, some of my peers have enjoyed numerous sexual experiences outside of marriage without any apparent consequences. Winner points out that the idea that "we will necessarily feel bad after premarital sex" forgets our sin nature.[9] Our depravity is good at smothering our conscience. Sinful sex, Winner says, will make some people feel fantastic.

The moral of these stories is not that sexual purity isn't worth it. But if our motivation for pursuing purity is personal fulfillment—the reward of married sex—then when the wedding never happens, our virginity is stolen from us, our marriage crumbles, our spouse dies, or sex fails to be nirvana, our conclusion *will* be that sexual purity isn't worth it.

In Psalm 73, Asaph laments that the wicked seem "always at ease," while his own obedience to God has not kept him from suffering:

> All in vain have I kept my heart clean
> and washed my hands in innocence. (Psalm 73:13 ESV)

He goes on to remember that the wicked will one day be "destroyed in a moment" (v. 19) and those who make God their refuge will ultimately be received to glory (v. 24). But he must grapple with the truth that we can't exchange our obedience to God for earthly reward. In our struggle to obey God, we may witness the wicked thriving, enjoying various pleasures, riches, and security, and wonder: Is it worth it?

Ultimately, reserving sex for marriage is worth it but because God is worth obeying. It's worth it because marriage is where sex belongs. Practicing sexual abstinence doesn't guarantee anyone marriage or awesome sex any more than taking up our cross and following Christ guarantees us health, wealth, or happiness. When we obey God for personal gain, Ferguson says, "Christ himself ceases to be central and becomes a means to an end."[10] Maybe one reason people leave the church is because we tell them purity is about sex, when really it should be about God.

SEX AS AN IDOL

As a teenager, I read my fair share of Christian romance novels. They were full of dramatic plot lines, one-room schoolhouses, and Canadian Mounties. They were stories where the word *sex* was never even mentioned, yet I got the distinct impression that being wanted sexually was the height of love and the solution to insecurity and rejection, that sexual intimacy solves loneliness. Christian dating books communicated a similar message: sinful lust was just a byproduct of singleness, and once I was married, I would be so sexually satisfied that lust would become a nonissue. Sex would solve it. Sex would solve so many things.

As a teenager during the era of purity culture, I internalized the message that sex was the most important aspect of marriage. Bombarded by articles urging Christians to "get married young" so they wouldn't explode from built-up passion, I began eagerly awaiting this promised happiness. I've since realized that, when we hold our joy captive until we get what we want, our discontentment looms larger and larger. Our idols grow taller. The imagination of the celibate is not challenged by the reality of sex—the reality that it is inconsistent and imperfect just like everything else after the fall—so the idea of sex can easily grow from a God-created good into a god of its own.

"I'm trying to think about how to articulate this," Sarah told me. "Sometimes it's hard for me to believe married friends when they tell me about the actual role sex plays in their marriage. Sex in marriage was emphasized *so dang much* that it ended up seeming like it was *the thing* that would make or break your marriage. I don't remember hearing even half as many talks on healthy relationships as I did about sex." Her experience resembles my own, and it was only after I was married that I realized that though sex is a part of the puzzle of marriage, it does not make up the whole picture.

For those who marry, the grand, all-consuming image of sex that purity culture paints for adolescents must reckon with the reality of sex in marriage. For some, this reckoning arrives the first night of their honeymoon. One man, Justin, told me that from everything he was taught growing up in evangelical purity culture, he was convinced his wife "would be some kind of sex goddess" and that sex in marriage would be the best experience of his life. However, the first night of their honeymoon "was filled with pain, discomfort, and tears." "It was world shattering," he said, "something we are still working through."

Joy Pedrow Skarka writes that, in one of her premarital classes, the instructor asked: "Do you have a vagina? Does he have a penis? Then sex will work." But after the elevator ride from their wedding reception to their hotel room, tears soon streaked her "wedding day make-up and forced [her] to whimper, 'We need to stop.'" The painful sex continued long after her honeymoon. She says, "I felt alone, with no one to turn to. So I turned to research. I searched everywhere for answers. And I discovered this: nearly three out of four women have pain during intercourse at some time during their lives. For some women, the pain lasts only for a time; for twenty to fifty percent of these women, the pain remains over time. Knowing this, I finally felt some peace. I decided to consult a doctor."[11]

Multiple women have told me about their struggles with vaginismus, a condition "characterized by involuntary contractions of the pelvic floor muscles that tighten the vaginal entrance, causing pain, penetration problems and inability to have intercourse."[12] But there are many causes of painful sex for women. One woman, Hannah, shared with me how her illness has affected her marriage, especially in regard to sexual intimacy:

> I have some level of pain every day. Some days I can ignore it, but some days it hurts even to be gently touched, even to put clothes on, and on those days, sex is impossible. Other days, I may not be in as much pain but the

pain I do have has exhausted me. And since most of my pain is in my abdomen, I have lost a great deal of strength in my core muscles, so any sexual activity usually is pretty low on the "active" side, for me.

Understandably, this has all been disappointing for my husband. But until a recent conversation, I had assumed that it was not just disappointing but devastating. Years ago, in a less healthy time in our marriage, my husband had told me that sex was the only way he received love from me. Though we've both grown since that time, the messages of purity culture allowed me to accept his claim without question and to hold onto it through the past year of my illness.

And yes, it's been a year of not very much sex. I agonized over this fact as if it were an indictment on my character. If sex was vital to men in general, and if sex was the only way my husband could receive love from me, it meant he had gone a year receiving very little love from his wife, and this was unforgivable. I had projected disaster on to his simple disappointment and assumed that his less verbally expressive personality meant that he was holding on to deep bitterness and anger at me for withholding something he desperately needed.

Painful sex is not the only unaddressed reality in purity books and conferences. Many developed exaggerated expectations as to the frequency of sex within marriage. Men were promised that they could have sex any time they wanted once married, and women were told that their husbands would want to have sex every time they caught a glimpse of their bare skin.

Years ago, I was chaperoning a senior trip, riding in a fifteen-passenger van with some of my female students. One of them spoke up: "May I ask you a personal question?" "Of course," I replied, hoping to be the cool teacher who was willing to talk about anything. "How many times a week do you and your husband have sex?" I immediately felt my face flush. I didn't want to tell her. When I was her age, I had been given an exaggerated version of sex in marriage. But married sex had proven to be like the rest of life, with its own ebb and flow, affected by things like going to work, paying bills, studying, getting colds and headaches, grading papers, helping at church, and keeping up with friends and family.

At the time she asked, I was still working through reality versus my unrealistic expectations, and I felt ashamed to respond. If asked this same question today, I would say: it's not about how often. It's not about keeping up with other couples. I'm not going to tell you a number, but rather this: that sex is about unity, not quantity.

In addition to the pressure placed on frequency, sex—and especially female virginity—was repeatedly portrayed in Christian books and at purity conferences as the greatest gift you could give your spouse. I thought sex would be my magical wifely power, able to comfort and cure anything that ailed my husband. Because I was told that he would want sex constantly, I experienced deep and unnecessary rejection when he wasn't in the mood. Men had been painted as sex machines, not human beings who experience tiredness, sickness, and stress, just like everyone else. Treating sex as the barometer for the health of one's marriage also neglects all the other intimacies and beauties beyond intercourse, like laughing together, teasing each other, supporting one another, taking one another's dirty dishes to the sink, talking late into the night about dreams and goals, and loving one another through words.

While the world might want sex to be unexpected, even reckless, Winner says that it is "the stability of marriage that allows sex to be what it is."[13] Sex is meant to take place in the context of commitment—lifelong commitment. Sometimes this means familiarity more than excitement, or security over the thrill of the unknown. Married sex can be many things: fun, disappointing, comforting, wild and passionate, or quiet and slow. Sometimes achieving intimacy in marriage feels effortless. Other times, it takes patience and a willingness to keep learning about one another.

When sex is the goal of marriage, it becomes easy to idolize. This idolatry is destructive to unity between husband and wife, reducing the beauty and mystery of a lifelong, whole-self union to just one aspect. And when sex is presented to singles as the reward for their purity, it can lead to frustration, depression, and bitterness. For years, it was dangled like a carrot above our heads, and many of us are still working to overturn the idol of sex in our lives.

SEX AS A RIGHT

When we talk about the "right to life" for the unborn or for refugees, we are talking about their right to breath, food, water, and safe shelter. We are talking about the things that people need in order to survive. When sex is portrayed as a physical necessity, it suddenly joins rank with air, food, and water as a human right. An extreme but logically consistent manifestation of this thinking are "Incels," the "involuntarily celibate" men who blame women "for denying them their right to sexual intercourse."[14] But while popular culture might equate sex with our need for breath, and purity culture might talk about married sex as a future promise, the biblical truth is that God does not owe any of us sex.

For men who read books like *Every Man's Battle*, sex in marriage might seem more like a physiological need than a physical desire. This turns the gift of sex that married couples get to give one another into a debt that they owe each other. And these teachings fail to recognize that sex in marriage is about selfless giving and receiving, not selfish demanding.

Many in the purity movement were assured that married sex would solve their struggles with sinful lust. When it didn't, some found it easier to blame their spouse rather than question the promise or admit that they were still dealing with sexual temptation. The idea of married sex as a lust antidote likely comes from 1 Corinthians 7, which tells husbands and wives "do not deprive each other" of sexual relations "so that Satan will not tempt you because of your lack of self-control" (v. 5) and which bids the unmarried and widows to marry "if they cannot control themselves . . . for it is better to marry than to burn with passion" (v. 9). If we fail to read passages like these beside the whole counsel of Scripture, we will walk away believing that sex becomes a right within marriage. But alongside calling spouses to give to one another sexually, Paul calls husbands to love their wives "just as Christ loved the church" and "gave himself up for her" (Ephesians 5:25). Can sacrificial, Christlike love include demanding sex or taking it by force? This cannot be what is meant by "conjugal rights" in 1 Corinthians 7:3 (ESV), when love and sacrifice are held up in Scripture as our highest Christian calling.

Lack of sex in marriage, whether due to sin, sickness, or distance, is never an excuse to seek sexual fulfillment elsewhere or demand it from one's spouse. A woman named Jennifer recently shared with me that her husband coerced her into performing sexual acts and raped her multiple times. He began seeing a Christian counselor, but instead of being rebuked for his sin against her, the counselor told him that he had biblical grounds to divorce her because she had "defrauded him of sex." In his mind, sex in marriage was his right—something he could take from his wife anytime he wanted, with or without her consent—which turned her from a precious gift into a sexual object, there to do his bidding. This is not what God desires for sex or marriage.

Dealing with these messages in marriage was one thing, but after my divorce I had to grapple with what it meant in a new season of singleness. Before my first marriage, I had desired sex as a virgin. Now I was single with the experience and memories of sexual intimacy with someone. If marriage flips a switch that turns sex into a physiological need, what are the divorced and widowed to do? The truth is, I don't believe in such a "switch." My desire for sex as a divorced single differed from my desire for sex as a single virgin, but I was asking the same question in both seasons: What do I do with all this longing?

One single woman I interviewed told me that in purity culture she always heard one's sex drive compared to hunger for food. "If sex was sustenance, then I was starving to death, and God was still telling me that I couldn't steal the hoagie from the shop window." She says she felt entitled to marriage and sex because she had faithfully practiced sexual purity, and she was "angry and confused" when neither showed up. But her story didn't end there. She went on to talk about her crisis of faith and the messages she had to question and grapple with in her singleness:

> It wasn't until I decided to imagine a good life for myself without a husband and accepted the possibility that I might never be married or have sex that I actually began to heal. I am now a 33-year-old virgin. I'm not lonely, angry, or confused anymore. I still struggle with lust, but it doesn't feel like my future is a desert because I don't have sex or romance. Now that I am no longer trying to manipulate Providence with my virtue, my relationship with God is vibrant and wonderful. I may get married one day, or maybe I won't—but I'm not putting my life on hold waiting anymore. I'm also still planning to stay a virgin until and unless I do get married.

In pointing out that sex is not a biblical right or a life-and-death need, I don't mean to downplay the significance of sexual desire. In her book, *Party of One: Truth, Longing, and the Subtle Art of Singleness*, Joy Beth Smith admits that "it's crushing to live under the constant weight of unmet desires."[15] Instead of continuing to promise future married sex to singles, Smith goes on to urge them to "actively cling to promises that *are* in Scripture; promises that God will never leave us, promises of his control in all things, promises of his goodness, promises that the trials of this world pale in comparison to the glory of what is to come."[16] I love that Smith uses the word *trials* here, because unmet sexual desires—whether in singleness or marriage—can be some of the heaviest burdens we carry. We can acknowledge this. We *should* acknowledge this, to ourselves, to God, and to others.

The lack of discussion about the trial of sexual thirst often leaves individuals to struggle alone. The subject of masturbation deserves a more nuanced discussion (which we'll get to in chapter 9), but for some people the motivation for this act comes from the idea they have the right to satisfy their sexual thirst and achieve orgasm. For singles, masturbation—sometimes accompanied by pornography—can be a way to experience the physical pleasure of sex while maintaining their celibate status. But does masturbation merely act as a placeholder until God gives an individual marriage?

One woman I interviewed said that her husband was taught that "once he got married, he would never struggle with [masturbation] anymore because he could have sex whenever he had the desire to masturbate." But a young, single man commented that his married friends have been surprised at how much they continue to struggle with lust, pornography, and masturbation in marriage. Masturbating or viewing pornography out of a conviction that sexual gratification is a human right makes sexual expression about one person: yourself.

If this attitude toward sex continues into marriage, it can make the effort it takes to know another person sexually feel more like a burden than a joy.

Married sex is not about effortless self-fulfillment. It involves two people, which means learning. Communicating. Failing. Laughing. Crying. Years of practice. Studying one another and putting your spouse above yourself. Should you pursue orgasm in marriage? Absolutely. Get creative. Be patient with one another. Expect bodies to change and prepare yourself to get creative again and again. Learn your spouse. Care about their pleasure. Help them learn about yours. But do not make orgasm the goal of sex. God-designed, holy, married sex is about union, intimacy, self-giving, and joy. When sex is viewed as a right within marriage, it becomes more about selfish demanding than selfless love. And when sexual gratification is depicted as a physical need, it becomes much easier for all of us, single or married, to excuse sexual sin.

HOW WE VIEW SEX MATTERS

Rebecca Lemke agrees that "variations of a 'prosperity gospel' are a common theme in Purity Culture," noting how this leaves individuals to deal with "mismanaged expectations."[17] We must acknowledge that, despite good intentions, false promises were made. Sex was used as a bargaining chip. And many of us went on to feel cheated and lied to as we watched those promises crumble or fail to ever materialize.

As a church, we must question any teachings that depict sex as a reward, a promise, or a need. We will not die from unmet sexual longings, and we can be sexually whole without being sexually gratified. Sex is a gift, not a right. It is temporary, not eternal (Matthew 22:30). Sex is both much more and much less than the idol we have created. And whether we're having great sex, disappointing sex, or no sex at all, we will eventually arrive at the same conclusion: sex is not God. It cannot be. It is not even *a* god, despite its many worshipers.

And, beloved, sex is not necessary for a full, God-honoring Christian life. Sex can be a great blessing, but consider too the gift the apostle Paul spoke of: how singleness and celibacy freed him to focus on Christ and his ministry. Think about spiritual heroes like Amy Carmichael or Rich Mullins who never married yet their lives still echo the gospel, long after their deaths.

We must take time to remind ourselves that sex—and indeed all creation—is for the glory of God. Sex can feel like such a fragile thing, wrought with hurt, anxiety, hope, and brokenness. It is so difficult to hand sex over to God, especially when it involves releasing our grip on dreams and longings we have held for years. We live under the curse, and God's good creation soon becomes twisted by our sin and selfishness. His gifts were never meant to be worshiped, but we exchange the truth about God for a lie and worship and serve the creation rather than the Creator (Romans 1:25). We need his mercy, his Word, and the local church as we wrestle with these truths, lies, and questions about sex. It takes courage to step out into the light.

DISCUSSION QUESTIONS

1. Do you view sex as a need? Why or why not? What is your biblical basis for this belief?
2. How would Scripture speak, directly or indirectly, to sexual practices such as masturbation? Pornography?
3. What would you tell someone who says that rape cannot exist inside marriage? How does Scripture support your answer?
4. In what ways has sexual sin and lust affected your relationships or interactions with others? How has it affected your relationship with God?

5. What are some practical ways we can work toward bringing the subject of sex out of the darkness and into the light in our churches and communities?
6. How have your views and expectations about sex changed? What brought about these changes?

ACTIVITY

Create a list with two columns. On one side, write down any lies and unbiblical beliefs you had in the past about sex. On the other side, list as many biblical truths about sex that you can think of. Once you've completed both sides, find a partner or get into a small group and discuss the lies and truths you each recorded. After discussing your lists, spend some time praying for one another, asking God to transform your thinking, renew your minds, and plant his truth deep within your hearts.

7

WHAT THE SEXUALLY ABUSED HEAR

It all started with a Google image search. I typed in *Bathsheba*, curious to see how artists and filmmakers had portrayed this infamous bathing beauty in biblical literature over the years. The images that popped up either presented her as an exhibitionist, bathing provocatively on a rooftop, or as a woman in love with a king, taking David's gentle, outstretched hand.

I felt righteous anger rising in my throat. Not one of them showed the trauma of a woman taken from her home. None of the images captured the fear on her face when she realized what she had been brought to the palace for. I clicked and scrolled, shaking my head. Then I shut my laptop and walked outside the common room at St. Mary's College in St. Andrews to call my husband.

"Honey, I think I'm going to change my dissertation topic." I went on to explain my new idea.

"I thought you were going to write about how the church needs to create more space for lament?" my husband practically pleaded.

"I know, I know, but then I started thinking about the ways that the church contributes to a culture that shames female victims of sexual abuse. . . ." I went on and on. He listened. He is such a good listener. At the very end I asked him: "How do you feel about me delving into this topic? I know you will carry the weight of my frustration and heavy heart."

He didn't fully understand the sudden switch, but neither did he hesitate to say: "Of course, baby. Go get 'em." And with that, seven months of research began over ways purity culture rhetoric harms female victims of sexual abuse.

Sexual abuse is about power. Because of this, there are victims of all ages and genders. We read in Genesis 39 about Potiphar's wife attempting to force Joseph into having sex with her. She abuses her positional power to try and manipulate Joseph, forcing herself on him. Luckily, he escapes. But instead of receiving justice, Joseph is thrown into prison when Potiphar's wife essentially "cries rape" and blames him. If you are a male victim of sexual abuse, your story matters, your pain matters, and I hope this chapter can provide some comfort.

But my focus here will primarily be on young women, who are the most common victims of sexual abuse. In their research, Justin and Lindsey Holcomb found that "girls ages sixteen to nineteen are four times more likely than the general population to be victims of sexual assault."[1] Because of this, and the ways purity rhetoric overwhelmingly holds women responsible for guarding sexual purity, women are the ones most often revictimized by purity culture.

PURITY AS WHOLENESS NEGLECTS THE ABUSED

"I was abused at the age of twelve," Amber told me, "by someone in authority over me. That's right about the time I was being introduced to purity culture. We watched a video of a woman holding up a paper heart then tearing it in half. Then she took a hammer to a beautiful vase."

"How did these teachings affect you, having suffered sexual abuse?" I asked her.

"Because of the timing and what I was being taught, for all of my teen years I believed I was unworthy. Unworthy of God's love, of my future husband's love, of my father's love. When things finally came to light at age sixteen, the reaction caused me to resent the church. I resented the leaders and my parents. They acted as if my abuse caused them more damage than me."

Amber is an adult now, and a Christian, with a baby she treasures and a husband she loves. I ache, listening to her story. I ache, imagining how small she must have felt. What does it feel like to be met with annoyance instead of compassion when you feel broken? To be made to feel like a burden, instead of receiving the help you need?

"The things I was told while being abused made me believe he was doing what I wanted and that it was out of love. There was also fear and threats. I saw him as someone who I should respect and listen to. Eventually I 'fell in-love' with him. I used to think, 'Now we have to get married!' I believed that I could only ever be intimate with my husband so of course marriage was the answer. I was twelve. I didn't realize that what was happening was not intimacy. I didn't know anything."

She didn't know anything except what she was told. And she was told that sexual impurity breaks a person, like a glass vase left in shards on the floor. I want to tell you that Amber's story is rare, but you know that it is not. I want to tell you that I have never heard about the church pressing in on the wound of sexual abuse, making it deeper, leaving an even bigger scar. But you know that isn't true either.

Sexual abuse is *common*, a word I hate to use about something that should never be normalized, expected, or overlooked. The Holcombs point out that, according to national statistics, "every two minutes, someone in the United States is sexually assaulted."[2] If it is happening this often in America, it is happening to individuals in our churches. And beloved, those who have been sexually abused are listening to the way we talk about purity.

At a Silver Ring Thing event, speaker Matt Webster destroyed the symbolic wooden heart of a male volunteer with a chainsaw and gave a piece to three female volunteers, explaining that sexual immorality leaves parts of your heart with different people.[3] The sexually promiscuous are left splintered, with just a jagged piece of their own heart to give to their future spouse. Some purity groups, like True Love Waits, attempt to distinguish between consensual sex and sexual abuse by acknowledging that "virginity that is taken away is not lost."[4] Despite this distinction, the image of a massacred heart remains.

Christine Joy Gardner recalls interviewing Rachel Hollister, a young Christian who rejoiced that, due to her commitment to sexual abstinence, she and her husband didn't have to deal with sexual memories of anyone else.[5] The idea of singles saving their "firsts" for marriage is not always limited to sexual intercourse. Sarah Mally says that she's talked to many couples who saved "their first kiss, even their first touch" for marriage.[6] While the goal of this rhetoric is to encourage young people to value sexual purity, it neglects the statistically high number of people who have had unsolicited sexual experiences and memories forced on them due to abuse.

There is wisdom in encouraging adolescents to think through what they share with others before marriage, but this elevation of "firsts" is more likely to discourage than inspire those who have been sexually abused and robbed of the chance to choose when and how to be touched. One woman told me how she must fight viewing herself as "damaged goods." She said: "I worried that people in the church would blame or judge me if they found out, and that really affected my relationships with other believers."

Another woman shared her story:

> When I was fourteen, an eighteen-year-old male targeted me on a family-oriented missions trip. This resulted in my first kiss, which in hindsight more closely resembled assault, and is one of the most shame-filled experiences of my life. The youth pastor of another church traveling with us found out, blamed me, then gave me the ultimatum of "either you tell your parents or I will." So I did, through tears, and my dad literally said the words, "You have dishonored me." I also experienced childhood sexual abuse by a relative, which I hadn't disclosed until adulthood, so that very much played into my understanding of sex and sexuality. Purity culture unwittingly told me I was already broken, yet simultaneously gave me a crushing weight of maintaining my own righteousness. By God's grace I have learned so much about his beautiful design, and I've been delivered from shame by the Savior who became it and scorned it on the cross for me. I've abandoned the "fine china" analogies and instead revel in being a jar of clay, which has been crafted and cared for by a perfect Potter, all for his glory alone.

Being sinned against sexually is devastating and life-altering. And the shame of what has been done to our bodies attempts to block our view of the cross. But our value cannot be splintered. We may *feel* shattered, but our worth remains intact. No matter what has been done to us, or what we have done to others, we are never less than image bearers of the holy God. Any message that downplays this truth is worth challenging. The belief that all people are created in the image of God—the *imago Dei*—is a theology worth fighting for.

RAPE CULTURE IN PURITY CULTURE

In 2014, Judge G. Todd Baugh sentenced the rapist of a teenager to "just 30 days in jail" because he thought the victim, age fourteen, looked older than she was, and he believed she was "as much in control of the situation" as the teacher who raped her.[7] Blaming female victims for being sexually assaulted is nothing new. In America, the solution to the widespread problem of rape on college campuses often involves teaching young women strategies to avoid getting raped.[8] Alexandra Brodsky, Yale Law School graduate and campaigner against sexual assault on college campuses, says that this approach will "often ease assailants' culpability" by focusing instead on what victims should have done to protect themselves.[9] This thinking, sometimes referred to as "rape culture," has elements in common with the way the American evangelical church has addressed sexual purity.

Rape culture is a social climate of victim-blaming. Some general examples of this would be people saying the following of a woman who has been raped: "She chose to wear that skirt." "She chose to walk down that alley." "She chose to go on a date with him." Some specific examples that I have heard over the years include: "Well, yes, she was raped, but she had been flirting with him before it happened." "Yes, she was sixteen, but she knew what she was doing when she wore those clothes and spent that much time alone with her teacher." "She is probably just exaggerating. Besides, you know her reputation."

Sadly, this mindset appears in purity rhetoric as well. The assumption is that if a man approaches a woman with lust, she must have played some role in provoking it. While purity teachings certainly address the actions of men, the focus on female responsibility can overshadow men's agency in cases of sexual abuse.

Abby Perry has been chronicling the abuse of men and women in the evangelical church, sharing their stories in her column "Prophetic Survivors" at *Fathom* magazine. She tells the story of Ruthy Nordgren, who "grew up without a television . . . dressed in long denim skirts and t-shirts that never showed more than two inches between her collarbone and neckline." When Ruthy was twelve, she was molested by teacher, Aaron Willand, of Grace Baptist Christian School. And when she was fourteen, Willand "repeatedly raped her."[10]

But Ruthy did not receive justice. When the truth came out about what Willand had done to Ruthy, "Pastor Jon Jenkins began to spread rumors about Ruthy," Perry writes. "He told congregants and staff members that Ruthy's doctor told her mom she wasn't a virgin, which prompted Ruthy to cry rape. He told other congregants and staff members that Ruthy was a troubled girl known for telling lies." Willand's wife also began rumors that Ruthy had seduced her husband. The stories spread throughout her school, through teachers and students, and Ruthy was labeled a "whore."

Perry also interviewed Jules Woodson, who was sexually abused by her youth pastor, Andy Savage, as a teenager: "One night, Andy offered to drive Jules home after spending time with her and other students at the church. But Andy passed the street leading to Jules's mom's house and took an unfamiliar turn. Jules assumed they were going to get ice cream. Instead, Andy drove down a dirt road until he reached a dead end. He stopped the car, unzipped his jeans, and asked Jules to perform oral sex on him."[11]

The purity movement tries to empower women to resist the pressure to be sexually active in a sex-saturated culture, but this empowerment also creates a realm where women take on moral responsibility for what happens to them sexually. In the case of Woodson, Perry writes that "she mustered up the courage to tell their associate pastor, Larry Cotton, who said he would handle the situation. Over the following weeks and months, leadership completely ignored Jules, implying she bore as much guilt as her youth pastor." Woodson's abuser went on "to pastor elsewhere for nineteen years."[12] Lord, have mercy.

Purity teachings about the moral responsibility of women and the nature of male sexual lust position women as the guardians of sexual purity, so that when sexual purity is violated, it is women who are first and foremost on trial. It would be failure enough if female victims of sexual assault saw themselves as absent from purity culture rhetoric. The problem is, they *do* see themselves, only erroneously, as the guilty party.

PROBLEMS WITH PURITY AS EMPOWERMENT

Journalist Danielle Young writes about being sexually assaulted during multiple celebrity interviews over the years, including by Reverend Jesse Jackson, and how she was uncomfortable but tried to laugh off the advances. From her youth, Young says she was taught to be aware of "dirty old men" but "not in a way that held them responsible." Instead, she was raised to redirect the sexual attention of men by dressing and acting in ways that would discourage their attention. Consequently, "when the unwanted sexual attention came," Young writes, "I blamed myself."[13]

Although it might be empowering for an individual to think of sexual abstinence as a choice, there are times when a person's agency is stolen from them through abuse. The emphasis on personal empowerment in purity rhetoric leads some victims of sexual assault to conclude they are guilty of not using their power to prevent their abuse. Coincidently, the message of female moral responsibility in purity campaigns and books leaves female victims to wonder, like Young, if they were responsible for what happened to them.

"Contrary to the fairy-tale narrative," Gardner points out that, in modern purity rhetoric, "it is the prince who needs protection."[14] When one gender is given greater moral responsibility, as women are in purity culture, it complicates culpability. The Holcombs point out that victims of sexual assault often have to deal with questions from those closest to them about their "role in the assault" or implications that they somehow "asked for it."[15] This, along with other misunderstandings about sexual assault, can leave victims feeling guilty for crimes committed against them.

I have never been raped. My stories are the ones every woman has her own version of. Stories about that man on the street who asked me to smile then called me a "bitch" under his breath when I failed to comply. Stories about my hands shaking while holding the gas pump, trying to avoid the unrelenting stare of the man next to me. Stories about trying to protect friends from sexually charged taunts and text messages from their boyfriends and coworkers. Stories about long nights of "weeping with those who weep"—with those whose lives have been forever changed by the self-serving actions of another. And a story about a time I went dancing.

I used to swing dance a lot in high school. It was a way to have fun with my friends without having to deal with drunk strangers or listen to dubstep. One night, when I was 18, my friends and I dressed up and headed out. We danced poorly and laughed loudly. A few hours in, one of my friends offered to show me how to dance to the blues.

He was a wonderful dancer, so I said yes. He pulled me into a smaller room where people were moving to sultry music in low light. He showed me a few moves, but I spent most of the time stepping on his feet. We laughed. We danced close. I trusted his company and his intentions.

After the song was over, before I had a chance to take a breath, another man in the room grabbed my hands and pulled me to his chest. His arms were like iron and I felt trapped against his body. I tried to push myself back to a comfortable distance but couldn't. So I spoke up: "That's too close."

Instead of easing up, he laughed at me and replied, tauntingly: "I saw you dance like this with him."

Shame flooded me. He was right. I had danced close—probably too close—with my friend. I had set the standard. I was getting what I deserved. So I endured an entire song, pushed up against a stranger who seemed thoroughly amused by my inability to break free. When the song ended, he released me and I bolted out of the room.

My story is mild in comparison to what many women experience. But that doesn't mean what happened was okay. I remember going to sleep that night convinced that I had done something terribly wrong. Somehow, I had invited that man's actions into my life.

This internal conflict not only speaks to the way abuse and sexual harassment are regularly excused and mocked today. It also reveals an issue with our functional theology: if we truly believe in the *imago Dei*—that all people are created in the image of God—then we must recognize that what some brush off as "boys being boys" is actually a perpetuation of abuse that insults the image of God.

Growing up, when I got into a fight, I was often told that "it takes two to argue." And it's true. Rarely is a problem between two people the result of just *one* person's sin. But when we apply this thinking to situations of abuse, it can create murky waters in which the abuser swims away undetected and the abused is left sitting in the muck, confused. In cases of sexual assault, this mindset is dangerous because it connects two truths that must remain separate.

We all "have sinned and fall short of the glory of God" (Romans 3:23). But this truth does not invite an abuser to justify their abuse. Neither should the doctrine of natural depravity be used by the church to excuse abuse. Love "always trusts, always hopes" (1 Corinthians 13:7) but must also "do what is just and right" (Jeremiah 22:3). God's love does not keep him from executing "justice for the oppressed" (Psalm 146:7 ESV). Our love shouldn't either.

At Christian youth camps and during school chapels, I heard the same message over and over again: men can't help their lust, but women can. Jonathan Trotter confirmed the proliferation of this wrong thinking in the church when he admitted: "I grew up learning of the guy's responsibility to not look, and that's great, but what I really heard A LOT about was the girl's responsibility to not be looked at."[16]

When we teach men that they can't control themselves, we demean their dignity as image bearers and give them a preemptive excuse to abuse others. When we teach women that men can't control themselves, we communicate that abuse is not only inevitable but acceptable. We tell them that sexual assault is their responsibility to prevent. What this communicates is that, if it happens, *he* was "being a guy" and *she* "should have known better."[17]

LADIES SHOULD KNOW BETTER

Jessica Valenti, author of *The Purity Myth,* remembers how the 2006 rape and murder of Imette St. Guillen was reported. NBC's Matt Lauer framed the story as a reminder to young women about the dangers of "a night out." CBS talked about "how women can stay safe," and one *Wall Street Journal* article was titled, "Ladies, You Should Know Better."[18] Valenti writes that responding to rape by advising women how to avoid getting assaulted is merely "victim blaming shrouded in empowerment rhetoric."[19]

Most of the Christian books I studied place the burden of responsibility on women if they are sexually harassed or objectified by men. In *Every Young Woman's Battle,* Arterburn and Ethridge include the story of Diana, who describes the experience she had with an eighteen-year-old man at a Christian winter camp when she was fourteen. "He touched me a lot," she said, and "I began to feel uncomfortable." When he pulled her tightly to his body and touched her buttocks, Diana says, "I wanted to be offended, but I knew I had led him on with my flirting."[20] The rhetoric of responsibility in some of these books instructs women to expect sexual harassment from men, leaving them with the weight of figuring out how to act, dress, and approach men in ways that discourage their lust.[21]

When I ask women what comes to mind when they think of biblical femininity, they often respond with words like *quiet*, *meek*, and *polite*. One woman shared: "Feeling compelled to be polite led to me being sexually assaulted—and then I still felt responsible."[22] The pressure to stay quiet and be polite doesn't just come from the church, nor has it been placed on women only. My husband reminded me of what happened to Harry Dreyfuss, the son of actor Richard Dreyfuss, when he was reading lines with his father and actor Kevin Spacey years ago. While his father was *in the room*, Spacey touched Harry's thigh. Despite repeated efforts to get up and sit somewhere else, Harry says that Spacey followed him and eventually succeeded in grabbing his genitals. "Looking into his eyes, I gave the most meager shake of my head that I could manage," Dreyfuss says. "I was trying to warn him without alerting my dad, who still had his eyes glued to the page. I thought I was protecting everyone. I was protecting my dad's career. I was protecting Kevin, who my dad surely would have tried to punch. I was protecting myself, because I thought one day I'd want to work with this man. Kevin had no reaction and kept his hand there. My eyes went back to the script and I kept reading."[23]

Often, sexual predators count on the silence that shock and embarrassment produce; they know that they will likely get away with it. Multiple women shared with me about being groped in church. For those who ask questions like, "Why didn't she just slap him and run away?" "Why didn't he call the police?" "Why didn't she scream?"—please understand that there is much more at play in situations of sexual assault and rape. In fact, Harry Dreyfuss provides a good explanation as to why so many victims are only just now coming forward. He points out that laughing off his assault and downplaying it seemed like the best way to handle it until he realized the serious nature of what had happened when others started coming forward with their stories of sexual abuse. "I did a lot of mental gymnastics to normalize my experience," Dreyfuss admits, thanking the women who, in sharing their stories, sparked the #MeToo movement and helped him see "that what was once treated as normal never deserved to be."

Sometimes my desire to believe the best about people keeps me from listening to the siren going off in my head, telling me to leave, run, or speak up. Sometimes trying to be polite puts me in a position to be taken advantage of. It's hard to spot harassment when we are taught to deny its existence until it's too late, when we are told to wait for a punch to be thrown before calling it abuse.

But it is not failing to love your neighbor to wait for the next elevator. It is not unkind to put out your hand when someone comes in for a hug. You are not failing to be a witness at work when you report your coworker for sexual harassment. You are showing respect for the *imago Dei* in everyone. If we believe it right to defend the dignity of those created by God, we need to be consistent and protect our own dignity as image bearers. This might mean allowing your status as a servant of Christ to trump your desire to please people (Galatians 1:10).[24]

There is often confusion about what constitutes sexual assault. Justin and Lindsey Holcomb's thorough definition is so helpful, as it includes "any type of sexual behavior or contact where consent is not freely given or obtained and is accomplished through force, intimidation, violence, coercion, manipulation, threat, deception, or abuse of authority."[25] This definition gives us a lens through which to view the stories we have heard and the experiences we have had. It takes courage to revisit situations we have brushed off or mislabeled, and it takes humility to challenge our misconceptions about what constitutes sexual assault. One place Christians can start is by revisiting the story of David and Bathsheba.

BATHSHEBA—AN UNRECOGNIZED VICTIM OF SEXUAL ABUSE

Growing up in the church, I never heard Bathsheba described as a victim of sexual abuse. She was at best careless, and at worst a seductress. I cannot provide an exhaustive discussion of how purity rhetoric influences our hermeneutics, but I want to dig briefly into this one example. The Christian authors I studied each had something to say about Bathsheba. I will examine their views alongside the arguments of scholars and writers of theology like Sarah Bowler, who believes that challenging Bathsheba's portrayal in the church is one small step toward correctly viewing sexual abuse against women today.[26]

"Uriah's wife." New Testament scholar Richard Bauckham notes how genealogies "evoke the narratives" of those named.[27] When we read these lists, certain names stop us in our tracks. We recognize them and immediately begin recalling their story. In Matthew's Gospel, Bathsheba is mentioned alongside Ruth, Rahab, and Tamar in the genealogy of Jesus. But unlike the others, who are called by name, Bathsheba is referred to as "the wife of Uriah" (Matthew 1:6 ESV).

While John Eldredge says in *Wild at Heart* that Bathsheba goes unnamed because God was disappointed with her,[28] Richard M. Davidson suggests the opposite. Bathsheba's presence in the genealogy of Christ, he says, depicts her as honored.[29] He observes that Bathsheba is referred to as "the wife of Uriah" in the 2 Samuel account as well, after the death of Uriah, which implies her "continued fidelity to her [first] husband."[30] Bauckham points out that the adultery was David's alone, as Bathsheba "could hardly have been expected to do other than obey the orders of the king."[31] While Eldredge views Bathsheba as displeasing to the Lord, indicating his corresponding belief that she was complicit in an affair with David, theologians like Bauckham and Davidson provide support for their conclusion that Bathsheba was an unwilling participant.

An unrecognized victim. But David is not just guilty of adultery. I believe he is also guilty of rape. Without directly accusing Bathsheba of sin, Harris and Arterburn and Stoeker fail to label the story in 2 Samuel 11 an instance of rape or sexual abuse. Harris writes that David "slept with" Bathsheba while Arterburn and Stoeker say "he went to bed" with her.[32] Even David Powlison, in his book on restoring the sexually broken, mentions what "was done to" Tamar by Amnon but describes David's actions against Bathsheba as something they "did together."[33]

One possible explanation for these interpretations has to do with the way rape was defined, culturally, during the time the Old Testament was written. Unless a woman was kicking and screaming while it happened and someone witnessed it, it was unlikely that her assault would be labeled rape. Alexander I. Abasili points out that there is "no clear evidence in the narrative that the messengers literally seized and dragged Bathsheba to the palace," in the 2 Samuel account.[34] However, Bowler notes that David was in a "position of power" while Bathsheba was "not in a position to choose" whether or not to be brought to David.[35] Davidson echoes this conclusion, calling what David did to Bathsheba an example of "power rape," where someone in authority abuses their power in order to victimize another person sexually, with or without their consent.[36]

One other possible explanation for Harris and Arterburn and Stoeker's interpretation is the phrase in 2 Samuel 11:4, "she came to him." Bauckham notes that even feminist scholar Elaine Wainwright attributes action to Bathsheba based on this verse, but he does not believe this action implies consent, as Bathsheba had only two choices, "obedience or certain disaster."[37] Bowler adds that there is no indication in the text that Bathsheba "knew why she was summoned."[38] In other words, just because someone doesn't put up a fight doesn't mean they weren't raped.

But more convincing is Bowler's main argument, which centers on the fact that David is the one held accountable for this sin.[39] When Nathan confronts David, he uses masculine pronouns, while Bathsheba is symbolized as an innocent, stolen lamb. God does not appear to hold Bathsheba responsible. Why would we?

Bathsheba's moral responsibility. Purity culture's emphasis on a female sexual responsibility shows up in Gresh's and Mally's interpretations of the story of David and Bathsheba. Gresh believes that Bathsheba mourned the death of Uriah because "in a way, it was her fault," since she and David "sinned together."[40] Mally goes so far as to call Bathsheba a "tool of the enemy to bring calamity into David's life." She believes that the warning for men not to "give [their] strength to women" in Proverbs 31:3 was written by Bathsheba, who "learned very painfully" the consequences of "moral failure."[41] While scholars such as George G. Nicol view Bathsheba as "calculating" and "deliberately provocative," ambiguity surrounding Bathsheba's responsibility dissolved for Bowler when she actually studied the text and became convinced of Bathsheba's innocence.[42]

Read through the lens of purity culture, the narration that from his roof, David "saw a woman bathing" (2 Samuel 11:2) recalls teachings on female modesty and men's susceptibility to visual stimuli. In that context, it becomes easy to categorize

Bathsheba as a temptress. But in examining the context of the passage, we remember that David is a king; a king who likely has a unique view into the homes of his subjects from his high castle. Bathsheba is not the scantily clad woman walking past men in her shortest skirt and brightest lipstick in hopes of being ogled; it's more likely that Bathsheba thought herself safe from prying eyes. And, to further crumble our original reading of the story, Bible scholars point out that Bathsheba may have actually been partially or fully clothed as she obeyed God in "ritual washing" from her "menstrual impurity."[43]

In regard to visual stimulation and sexual self-control, much is revealed by comparing the two men in the story. While David chose to peer in on a private moment and then satiate his sexual lust by "forcing Bathsheba into his bed," Uriah, who knew intimately of his wife's beauty, practiced sexual self-control, finding it "dishonorable to sleep in his own house with his wife while his comrades sleep outdoors on the battlefield."[44] After raping Bathsheba and discovering that she was pregnant as a result, David gave Uriah the chance to go home and sleep with his wife, hoping this would hide the truth of what he had done. But Uriah's decision to honor his duty dispels the purity myth that men reach a point where they are helpless to resist their sexual urges. He had been away from his wife at war for some time, and he still refused David's invitation to go home and sleep with Bathsheba for a night (2 Samuel 11:7, 11).

RECOGNIZING THE BATHSHEBAS IN OUR MIDST

Powlison observes that "Tamar bore no blame for what Amnon did to her," and yet she still wrestled with "shame, grief, dismay, and isolation."[45] If Tamar struggled with shame when what she endured was labeled "rape" in 2 Samuel 13, how much must the Bathshebas in our midst wrestle with false guilt and blame for the sexual abuses they have endured without ever being declared innocent. The Holcombs note that too many victims of sexual abuse believe "they didn't do enough to stop the assault," or that they were at fault for being "at the wrong place, at the wrong time, with the wrong people."[46] An astounding number of individuals experience sexual abuse without any form of justice or recognition as victims.

As a largely unrecognized victim of sexual abuse, Bathsheba demonstrates the importance of a clearer definition of sexual assault. If men are to be truly held accountable for their sexual actions, and female victims of abuse are to be recognized as true victims, we must stop labeling sexual assault as "lust gone wild" and understand it as the act of "power and control" it truly is.[47]

Gresh, Arterburn, and Ethredge, the same authors who failed to see Bathsheba as a victim of sexual abuse, also categorized instances of sexual assault in their books as stories where women failed to properly guard their bodies.[48] Once Christians can recognize what David did to Bathsheba as rape rather than a story about "predatory women" or Bathsheba's failure to guard herself sexually, they can begin to recognize female victims of sexual abuse outside and within the church.[49]

Caryn Tamber-Rosenau draws attention to the fact that Bathsheba is never blamed or held responsible for her sexual experience with David in the biblical texts.[50] She notes that "even when David and Bathsheba's first son dies," Nathan points to David as the one responsible, and therefore any blame placed on Bathsheba is the result of "postbiblical interpretations."[51] These postbiblical interpretations have an influence on how Christians respond to cases of sexual abuse, including those that take place in our own churches. Reevaluating stories like Bathsheba's can reveal errors in our thinking and theology and aid the church in recognizing victims today.

MOVING FORWARD

In his religious studies course, Jeremy Posadas has a strategy to help his students grasp the concept of rape culture.[52] It is simple—something any of us can do. He has his students read the stories of people who survived sexual abuse. This practice alone—of listening to survivors—could have a transformative impact on purity leaders who have treated female victims of sexual abuse as an anomaly rather than a significant percentage of their audience. It could change the way the church treats survivors who come forward. It could help the abused experience the comfort of community, support, and the pursuit of justice. And it could change the way we talk about sexual purity as the measure of one's worth and value. Stories have the power to disarm. To open blind eyes.

One benefit of the #MeToo movement is that these stories are more accessible now than ever. You can watch former gymnast Rachael Denhollander testify in court against convicted child molester Larry Nasser. Denhollander was the first of many victims to publicly accuse Nasser, and she did not mince her words or shrink from describing Nasser's abuse against her. Denhollander, a strong Christian, also took time to call him to repentance and to forgive him, saying: "I pray you experience the soul crushing weight of guilt so you may someday experience true repentance and true forgiveness from God, which you need far more than forgiveness from me—though I extend that to you as well."[53] You can read Abby Perry's "Prophetic Survivors" series. You can watch Jules Woodson respond in the *New York Times* to her abuser's "confession" to his church congregation, where he called the sexual assault against her a "sexual incident."[54] And most of all, you can listen when those around you open up about what they have been through.

Why is it important to recognize victims? This is the question so often at the heart of our hesitation. Can't we just move on from these things? What good does it do to dwell on who did what? Powlison points out that our sins and the sins committed against us are often entangled. It isn't always clear where one ends and the other begins. But I believe that culpability is worth untangling. Here's why.

First, justice matters to God. We won't all receive justice this side of heaven, but the church must set the example when it comes to reporting cases of sexual abuse. The vulnerable often seek safety in our pews, buildings, and Bible studies. We have the responsibility to protect them and to handle their stories with care. This includes but is not limited to reporting abuse to the proper legal authorities *outside* the church or Christian organization. This must be our first response.

In the #MeToo and #ChurchToo movements, we have seen that the church and Christian institutions too often fail to achieve legal justice for the abused because they try to handle situations "in-house." Sadly, some have neglected to report abuse out of a desire to protect the reputation of church leaders, institutions, and denominations, at the expense of the vulnerable. Beloved, this ought never be. The job of the church is not to play judge and jury while ignoring the laws of the land. We help victims legally, and then we continue to care for their emotional, physical, and spiritual well-being in the long-term recovery of sexual abuse.

The other reason blame is worth untangling is that we cannot be forgiven of sins we didn't commit. Powlison comforts victims of sexual abuse with these words:

> The Lord addresses the fainthearted in a very different way than he addresses unruly and lustful desires. When you are gripped with apprehension, or you doubt that your Father could ever love you, or you're confused about how to think and what to do, or you flinch at the memory or possibility of being harmed, he simply says, "I am with you. Do not be afraid. I know what you are facing. I will

> never leave you or forsake you." Fears, shame, confusion, a sense of abandonment, and painful self-condemnation can continually darken the human heart. Fears are false prophets, breathing threats and prophesying disaster.[55]

Too many victims of sexual abuse blame themselves for what happened. This false guilt does not produce the righteousness of God. Peace cannot be achieved on a foundation of lies. God holds individuals responsible for their own sins. And, goodness knows, we each have enough of those to fill our daily prayers. Abuse victims wrestling with deep shame need to grasp their victimhood so they can understand the difference between what they have done and what has been done *to* them. This may take time. There is no time clock or foot tapping. But ultimately, healing springs from the soil of truth.

DISCUSSION QUESTIONS

1. What do you think of when you hear the term "rape culture"? Do you believe that it exists within the church?
2. How do you feel about the practice of teaching women how to avoid being raped?
3. What is the balance between loving our neighbor and protecting ourselves?
4. What were you taught about Bathsheba? Did you view her as a seductress, a romantic lead, or a victim of rape?
5. The idea of sexual consent is being emphasized in modern American society. Should the church be talking about consent too? Why or why not?
6. What can we take away from the story of Joseph and Potiphar's wife?
7. What can we take away from the story of David and Bathsheba?

8. This chapter does not thoroughly address how the local church should respond if someone shares that they have experienced sexual abuse. To begin this vital discussion, I recommend the resources available at churchcares.com and netgrace.org.

ACTIVITY

This chapter raises difficult issues and questions. End your time by praying together for your local church (and, if applicable, denomination), that God would bring healing and justice to the abused, grant your church leaders wisdom and compassion for victims, and that any sexual abuse taking place within the church would be revealed and rooted out.

8

SUBMITTING TO GOD'S SEXUAL ETHIC AS EMBODIED SOULS

The forgiveness of God is gratuitous liberation from guilt. Paradoxically, the conviction of personal sinfulness becomes the occasion of encounter with the merciful love of the redeeming God.

Brennan Manning

What does sexual flourishing look like for the Christian? For the young married couple in their twenties, the divorced father of three, or the same-sex attracted teen? What does it mean to appreciate our God-given sexuality while submitting expressions of it to his authority and good plan? Allowing culture to dictate our response is not the right answer. But allowing the purity movement, a Christian subculture that we created and allowed to shape our worldview, isn't the answer either.

My dad used to say at the end of almost every sermon: "Don't take my word for it. See for yourself." Then he would hold up his Bible as if it were a road map, bidding the congregation to take up this precious gift. As you read my fumbling attempt to summarize God's sexual ethic, please don't take my word for it. Open his book. Press into the Scriptures. Ask the Holy Spirit to give you eyes to see and ears to hear. Open it while alone, in prayer. Open it with others, in study. Open it often and let it be a light to your feet.

GOD EMBODIED

One of the realities we discover as we dig into the Bible is the miraculous embodiment of God in Jesus. Holiness took on flesh. The light that made Moses' face shine, the whirlwind that approached Job—this God became human. He had a body. *Has* a body. And I don't say this to be crass but to take God at his Word: Jesus was a sexual being.

Joy Beth Smith bravely presses into this truth, noting that during his time on earth Jesus had to "figure out his body and control its reactions as a young boy and later as an adult, even as women knelt at his feet or tugged on his robes."[1] Why does the fact of his embodiment make us uncomfortable? I believe it is because we struggle to separate sexuality from sexual sin, and therefore it is hard for us to imagine that Jesus could be both sexual and sinless. Smith calls this unhelpful union a "man-made bridge."[2] We built it together, and together we must knock it down, starting with the fact that sex is a God-created, God-imagined good.

THE ORIGINAL SIN

Sex existed before the fall. It was not the original sin and, despite centuries of artistic depictions of Eve as a seductress, neither was it the first temptation. Sex was part of God's plan from the very beginning, part of his creation, and as Nancy Pearcey points out, it was part of what God pronounced "very good."[3] Genesis 2 records the creation of Eve who, after being formed, would "become one flesh" (v. 24) with Adam—a phrase used in Scripture to describe both the mystery of the marriage covenant as well as the physical act of sexual intercourse (1 Corinthians 6:16). In the beginning, sex was good. God made it and those expressing it were united in the covenant of marriage.

We see that goodness, that freedom and intimacy, in Genesis. Adam and Eve were both fully naked and "they felt no shame" (Genesis 2:25). Can you imagine? No insecurity. No blushing. Just pure, uninhibited sexual unity between husband and wife. No bed sheets were needed. No window shades pulled down. They enjoyed sex freely, in front of the birds and the bees, knowing God could see them and was completely unbothered by it. In the garden, sexuality was free from shame.

It was also free from sin. What has happened since that time in the garden? When did sex get distorted? Perverted? When did it turn from a source of joy to a source of shame and brokenness? We know the answer. We have read about the tree and the serpent and the fruit. But what really happened on that fateful day when sin entered the world happened after Satan whispered four words to Eve: "Did God actually say . . . ?" (Genesis 3:1 ESV). The first temptation of humankind was to disbelieve God. Sin—sexual and otherwise—always begins by doubting God's words. After Eve and Adam ate the fruit from the forbidden tree, sin was made manifest in the form of bodily shame. Genesis 3:7 records: "Then the eyes of both were opened, and they knew that they were naked. And they sewed fig leaves together and made themselves loincloths" (ESV). They didn't feel the need to cover their hands or feet. They covered their genitals. Sexual self-consciousness entered the world that day.

And self-consciousness and self-worship go hand in hand. Daniel Darling believes that "self-worship was the seduction offered in Eden."[4] Looking at the story this way, we see temptation to sin not as low-hanging fruit, dangled by a God who likes to watch humans squirm, but as humankind's outright rejection of God in favor of self. This is what Adam and Eve were really choosing over obedience to God. Look at what the serpent went on to say: "God knows that when you eat from it your eyes will be opened, and you will be like God, knowing good and evil" (Genesis 3:5).

Adam and Eve had everything they needed to flourish—physically, emotionally, and sexually. The world and everything in it were about God's glory, and the Garden of Eden was a place where his image bearers could worship him just by enjoying his beautiful earth, each other, and sweet intimacy with their Creator and friend. All their needs were met. Until the day Satan reminded them that they were not God.

And the desire to be the god of your life—of your sexuality—is still a serpent in the ear, a lie in the heart. We are not above falling for the original sin over and over again. Recognize that self-worship is behind every act of disobedience, even the ones we try to justify or minimize. Every time we sin, we are saying, "I choose to be my own god."

The fall destroyed perfect intimacy with God and with one another—a destruction that we are still recovering from, accompanied by longings that will not be satiated this side of heaven. Created good, our bodies now live under the weight of that day, along with the rest of creation, groaning and longing to be made new. When we sin sexually, it is not because sexuality is corrupt or because sex is evil, but because *we* are corrupt, continually exchanging the truth of God for lies (Romans 1:25).

WHAT WE DO IN THE DARK

During a unit on the theology of surveillance at the University of St. Andrews, my classmates and I discussed the watchful eyes of God. The reverberating response in my discussion group was that God doesn't need to watch everything, and that there are some places his eyes shouldn't go. When pressed, it became clear that these comments were generally referring to what happened in the bedroom.

I can hear Whitney Houston singing: "His eye is on the sparrow / And I know He watches over me." These words bring comfort in certain contexts, but in others we find ourselves wishing that God wasn't quite so omnipresent. All the same, we cannot hide from him:

> Where can I go from your Spirit?
> Where can I flee from your presence?
> If I go up to the heavens, you are there;
> if I make my bed in the depths, you are there.
> If I rise on the wings of the dawn,
> if I settle on the far side of the sea,
> even there your hand will guide me,
> your right hand will hold me fast.
> If I say, "Surely the darkness will hide me
> and the light become night around me,"
> even the darkness will not be dark to you;
> the night will shine like the day,
> for darkness is as light to you. (Psalm 139:7-12)

God not only sees how we treat sex in our hearts, our bodies, and our minds, he also cares how we treat it. And he knows we need Jesus' blood to cover our sins—including the sexual ones. Paul reminds us: "You were bought at a price." How do we, as Christians, respond to such a gift? By glorifying God in our bodies—and with all our heart, soul, mind, and strength (1 Corinthians 6:20; Mark 12:30).

Our sexuality is not independent from God or our call to love our neighbors. How we treat sex affects those around us. When we view pornography, for example, we are not just sinning against God, we are sinning against the people in that image or movie, against our spouse (if we are married), and against other image bearers of God who have become depersonalized and objectified as a result. When we lust after someone in our heart, it may seem like a private sin, but it is nevertheless against a real person. Treating them selfishly in our minds is bound to show up in the way we treat them in person.

A woman I interviewed confessed that her private sexual fantasies trained her brain to "see men as objects." Even when an individual wasn't the object of her lust, she says that her devotion to habitual masturbation had created a selfish mindset. She began viewing other people as existing to meet her emotional needs. "When they didn't say the exact things I wanted to hear or do the exact things I wanted them to do in order for me to feel loved or accepted," she withdrew, became angry, or picked a fight.

There are no hidden or harmless sexual sins. We have been called out of darkness into his marvelous light (1 Peter 2:9). Even the most discreet sexual sin will have its effect on our intimacy with God, our church, and our witness, which is why God calls us to step into the light of his grace and forgiveness—day by day, minute by minute. And when we live in this liturgy of repentance and forgiveness, we will not despise the eyes of God.

DISTORTIONS IN HOLINESS

As you may be aware, I am not the only one reevaluating the messages of evangelical purity culture. Two of the most recent books on the topic contain stories of times the authors had sex with their boyfriends. They both deem these instances of extramarital sexual intercourse good and holy—a time of deep communion with God.

Linda Kay Klein, who describes herself as a Christian standing "outside of the hand [she] grew up in," writes:

> I was twenty-six. In a quaint Japanese hotel room with a long-term boyfriend that I was certain I would marry,

> in the way in which we are absolutely certain of just about everything in our twenties. And the sex/shame brain trap just . . . broke. I prayed the whole while. Thanking God for the moment, the man, and most of all, that I might finally be free. And a holy presence filled the room. My boyfriend startled. "Is someone else in here?" He asked. "Yes," I answered him.[5]

Similarly, Lutheran pastor Nadia Bolz-Weber writes about a time after her divorce:

> When I started seeing my boyfriend, I felt connected to him and to my body and my desires and my erotic nature in a deep way. It was like an exfoliation of my entire spirit. It softened me and opened my heart and cleared away the gunk in my head. It was good. Not perfect. *Good.* Good like bodies. Good like chocolate cake. Good like when God saw what God made, and God looked at it and said it was good.[6]

Bolz-Weber insists that "when two loving individuals, two bearers of God's image, are unified in an erotic embrace, there is space for something holy."[7]

Beloved, do not be deceived by such thinking. The gospel of self is everywhere, and it tastes sweet, like wine. Which is why we must drink all the more deeply of God's Word—so that our hearts are not deceived: God is about his glory. God loves you, and your highest good is to be about his glory too.

The gospel of self continues throughout the ages, and there are pastors, writers, and theologians who continue to infuse this false gospel into books and sermons alongside Scripture, making it difficult to sort out truth from lies, right from wrong, holy from wicked. But God urges us:

> Brothers and sisters, in view of God's mercy . . . offer your bodies as a living sacrifice, holy and pleasing to

> God—this is your true and proper worship. Do not conform to the pattern of this world, but be transformed by the renewing of your mind. Then you will be able to test and approve what God's will is—his good, pleasing and perfect will. . . .
>
> Love must be sincere. Hate what is evil; cling to what is good. Be devoted to one another in love. Honor one another above yourselves. . . .
>
> Let us behave decently, as in the daytime, not in carousing and drunkenness, not in sexual immorality and debauchery, not in dissension and jealousy. Rather, clothe yourselves with the Lord Jesus Christ, and do not think about how to gratify the desires of the flesh. (Romans 12:1-2, 9-10; 13:14)

There is forgiveness at the cross for every sin. And we can grow from our mistakes, learn from our failures, and even look back with thankfulness at times when God showed mercy to us despite our disobedience. But when we start calling "holy" what God calls sinful, we have ceased to honor him. We have misunderstood what holiness means.

Holiness is not premarital sex without shame. Holiness is God, the Lord Almighty, who was, and is, and is to come (Revelation 4:6-8). Paul is swift to deal with sexual immorality within the church. It is not tolerated. In Corinth, a man was having sex with his mother-in-law. Paul heard about this, that the church not only failed to confront this man's sin but seemed to take pride in letting it continue. He did not mince his words: "Your boasting is not good. Don't you know that a little yeast leavens the whole batch of dough? Get rid of the old yeast, so that you may be a new unleavened batch—as you really are. For Christ, our Passover lamb, has been sacrificed. Therefore let us keep the Festival, not with the old bread leavened with malice and wickedness, but with the unleavened bread of sincerity and truth" (1 Corinthians 5:6-8).

If he were alive today, Paul would have been less concerned with sexual immorality in Hollywood or in politics and more concerned with those who claim the name of Jesus engaging in unrepentant sexual sin. Sexual sin should not be allowed to flourish in our churches. Whether that sin takes the form of sexual harassment, premarital sex, pornography addiction, or something else, it should be rooted out and dealt with in truth, wisdom, and love, not hidden away, excused, or praised.

Jude calls us to "show mercy, mixed with fear—hating even the clothing stained by corrupted flesh" (Jude 23). How might this relate to our interactions with those who are caught up in sexual sin? Theologian Michael Green says that believers have the privilege of offering, through Christ, "a robe of righteousness for the man clothed in filthy rags (cf. Isaiah 61:10)" but that "once he begins to revel in the filthy garment, once he tolerates it and toys with it, he ceases to be a useful servant of Christ at all. Once he treats sin as normal and commonplace, he is on the way to betraying the gospel."[8]

Does this mean that the merciful heart, gentle with love, is more susceptible to downplaying sin? I don't think so. But if I am honest, I must admit that my genuine mercy often gets twisted up in my desire for human praise. I may start out with the right motives, but somewhere along the line my desire to *be* loving morphs into a desire to *seem* loving. And I can start to soften the edges of sin, calling what God has deemed filthy, clean. In doing so, I fail to love God and my neighbor.

There will come a day when our desire to seem loving will make war with our desire to be loving. On that day, it is only through the power of the Holy Spirit that any of us will stand on solid ground. Pray now for that strength. Our Christian calling is to walk side by side with truth and love. Selfish mercy cowers away from naming sin. It fears people more than God. But true mercy knows that what each of us needs more than anything else is the gospel—and the rivers of living water that rush in when we recognize ourselves as sinners and Jesus as Savior.

THE SOURCE OF OUR PURITY

As much as we might prefer theology to come in black and white, our relationship with sin is complicated. In Romans 6, Paul says that Christians are those who have "been set free from sin" (v. 7). We have died to it and are no longer sin's slave. But in the very next chapter, Paul points out that, although he delights in God's law, sin continues to wage war inside him. He admits: "Although I want to do good, evil is right there with me" (Romans 7:21) and laments that, rather than doing good, he often does the very evil he hates (v. 19). But here is hope at the end of Paul's admission: "Thanks be to God, who delivers me through Jesus Christ our Lord!" (v. 25).

God's sexual ethic is first meant to reveal our sin as "utterly sinful" (Romans 7:13) and to devastate us into acknowledging our need for a Savior. Jesus' Sermon on the Mount reveals us all as sexual sinners: the virgins, the serial adulterers, the porn addicts. We all fall short of God's command to see one another as brothers and sisters in all purity. The main point is not pursuing sexual purity but recognizing our impurity and our desperate need for Christ. So many of us walked right past the gospel on our way to a purity conference. Our parents and youth leaders were so concerned about our budding sexuality, scrambling for direction and wisdom, that some of us ended up signing abstinence pledges before falling on our knees in repentance. We wore purity rings as badges of honor, forgetting that it is Jesus who cleanses us from all unrighteousness.

The Christian pursuit of sexual purity is biblical, but it *must* flow out of a recognition that it is Jesus who makes us pure. Otherwise, we become Pharisees. And the Pharisee inside us will eventually ask: Why pursue sexual purity if it does not earn us favor with God? Sinclair Ferguson notes that the "medicine the gospel prescribes" for this kind of thinking is "understanding and tasting union with Jesus Christ himself."[9]

Pursuing sexual purity to earn God's approval is just one of our many misguided motivations. Pursuing sexual purity to earn blessings like marriage, sex, and babies is also misguided. Just like the legalist, the believer in purity prosperity will eventually ask: If disobeying God's sexual ethic doesn't always result in immediate physical consequences, and if pursuing sexual purity doesn't guarantee a happy marriage, great sex, and lots of babies—why pursue it? Tim Keller, summarizing John Owen, reminds us that obedience is not "simply a way to avoid danger and have a good life" but is "a way to love and know Jesus for who he is."[10] We don't earn Jesus. We receive him as a gift. Obedience, sexual or otherwise, is one way we get to love and worship the God who rescued us.

COUNTERCULTURAL TRUTH

Pastor and author Scott Sauls recently addressed the swinging pendulum of responses that exist in the church when it comes to sexual ethics. On one side, there are those who hold firmly to all of Scripture, but lack "pastoral compassion, empathy, and grace." On the other side, there are those who show mercy and kindness but are often "lacking in biblical fidelity." He believes that "the sex question is one that sincere believers must wrestle with. We must remain committed to being counter-cultural where the culture and the truth are at odds with one another."[11]

In contrast, Nadia Bolz-Weber tells the story of Cecilia, a parishioner who grew up during the evangelical purity movement and, like so many of us, committed to saving sex for marriage. After walking away from the church in her late twenties, Cecilia started dating her boyfriend and having sex. He eventually cheated on her, and she was left brokenhearted, wondering if his decision had anything to do with her sexual inexperience. Bolz-Weber concludes that Cecilia was "robbed" by the church, who "took away over a decade of her sexual development." Bolz-Weber and Cecilia both admit to being angry. Their anger is not at the boyfriend who cheated but at the church for keeping Cecilia from the chance to gain the "kind of wisdom that comes from making her own choices, from having lovers, from making mistakes, from falling in love."[12]

Essentially, Bolz-Weber believes that the church failed Cecilia because it upheld God's sexual ethic. I too believe that the church has failed in its approach to sexual purity. We have turned sex and marriage into household idols. We have talked about virginity as if it were a means of salvation. We have adopted a version of the prosperity gospel. We have shamed victims of sexual abuse for actions committed against them. We have dehumanized men and women by talking about them as pitfalls and obstacles instead of as image bearers. We have allowed cultural tides to carry us away from the revealed Word of God. But, beloved, upholding God's command to keep sex within marriage has not been one of our failings. And I will stand by all the other antiquated sticks-in-the-mud who still remember Jesus' words in John 14:15: "If you love me, you will obey me" (WE).

SEXUAL FLOURISHING AND THE CHRISTIAN

How can a Christian flourish sexually according to God's sexual ethic? By surrendering, body and soul, to God the Creator and lover of our souls. By praising him with every fiber of our being—soul, mind, and body—and by treasuring Jesus himself as the gift, the benefit, of life with God. Ferguson points out that the serpent's temptation in the garden was "an assault on both God's generosity and his integrity." Satan was lying to Adam and Eve so that they would separate God's command from "God's gracious person."[13] God's call to sexual purity is not separate from his love for you. Remember that.

We don't like to talk about obedience. But the gospel wouldn't exist without it. Philippians 2:8 says of Jesus:

> And being found in appearance as a man,
> he humbled himself
> by becoming obedient to death—
> even death on a cross!

Jesus lived a life of obedience—including sexual obedience—in this flesh. He felt the ache of longing, the grief of losing, the joy of friendship, the temptation to reject God's voice. We are not alone in this body of flesh. God understands intimately and commands lovingly. Through new life in Christ, we who "once chose to be slaves of sin" are now free to obey God with our whole heart (Romans 6:17 LB). When self-worship changes our "Yes, Lord" into "Why not?" we must ask ourselves this question about the embodied Christ: Did what Jesus do in his physical body matter to God?

Yes. It is possible to appreciate sex, honor bodies, and love one another without rejecting God's sexual ethic. There is no one who cares more about our bodies than God. He created them—knit them together in our mother's womb. He grows them, cares for them, sympathizes with their weakness through the embodied Jesus. And he has promised that he will one day resurrect them. God's care for and lordship over our bodies is reflected in 1 Corinthians 6:13-20:

> The body, however, is not meant for sexual immorality but for the Lord, and the Lord for the body. By his power God raised the Lord from the dead, and he will raise us also. Do you not know that your bodies are members of Christ himself? Shall I then take the members of Christ

> and unite them with a prostitute? Never! Do you not know that he who unites himself with a prostitute is one with her in body? For it is said, "The two will become one flesh." But whoever is united with the Lord is one with him in spirit. Flee from sexual immorality. All other sins a person commits are outside the body, but whoever sins sexually, sins against their own body. Do you not know that your bodies are temples of the Holy Spirit, who is in you, whom you have received from God? You are not your own; you were bought at a price. Therefore honor God with your bodies.

Ferguson points out that "it was not legalism for Jesus to do everything his Father commanded him. Nor is it for us."[14] Sex that honors God is practiced and celebrated within the covenant of marriage between one man and one woman. It is precisely the fact that men and women are different that makes their coming together as one through sex in marriage such a beautiful mystery. The communication it takes. The intentionality and patience. It is their commitment to monogamy in marriage, to forsaking all others, that speaks to an even greater covenant. And the possibility of procreation, that a husband and wife's sexual union can create new life, is unique to heterosexual sex and provides us with modern-day miracle after modern-day miracle. Yesterday, my friend grabbed my hand and held it across her pregnant belly. I felt a kick from the little life inside her, and I stood in awe over God's design.

God created sex to be experienced between one man and one woman in the covenant of marriage *for our flourishing*. Not only for the continuation of the human race and unity between husband and wife but for the whole church, as a living illustration of Christ's love for us. If you are not married, the covenant of marriage, lived out around you, is meant to help you flourish. And you don't ever have to be a bride or a groom to experience covenant love, as every member of the church is bound to Christ, nourished and cherished by him, in holy union (Ephesians 5:29).

Still, our heads spin with the cultural questions of the day, the people we love, and the things we want. The serpent's words appear on our own tongue: "Did God really say . . . ?" What about the engaged couple? What about two consenting men? What about me and my boyfriend, once we feel safe and ready? We love each other. Isn't that what matters?

Many modern theologians would say yes. In *Shameless,* Bolz-Weber says that "we should not be more loyal to an idea, a doctrine, or an interpretation of a Bible verse than we are to *people.*"[15] While this might sound loving, and even remind us of the second greatest commandment, it ultimately dethrones God. It plays the soundtrack to the original sin on repeat, setting us up as the gods of our own lives. When Bolz-Weber explained some of the meaning behind the vagina statue she created, she said she wanted it to declare to the world: "This part of me is mine and I get to determine what is good for it and if it's beautiful and how I use it in the world."[16]

In contrast, Tish Harrison Warren, an Anglican priest, points out that yonic (vagina-shaped) imagery has been in the church for a long time. Because this distinctly feminine shape represents birth, it has been used in the design of baptismals, which are meant to represent our new life (or "rebirth") in Christ. Rather than acting as statements of autonomy, Warren says these yonic baptismal fonts declare "a rejection of self-constructed morality. They remind us that, if we are baptized, Jesus calls the shots about morality and the right use of our bodies."[17]

It is not our lack of sexual exploration or liberation that should grieve us but the years that our lusts have eaten, the time we could have spent surrendered to Christ, enjoying intimacy with him; the heart space that could have been filled with his promises, that we instead spent on rebellion and lesser things. *God, give us courage and strength to uphold your vision for our bodies, our relationships, and our love. Help us to flourish in obedience to you.*

DISCUSSION QUESTIONS

1. Why do you think God created sex? What is its purpose?
2. What does sexual flourishing look like for the married Christian? The single Christian? The same-sex attracted Christian? The widowed or divorced Christian?
3. Do we need a new Christian sexual ethic? If so, what should it be? If not, why not?
4. How should we deal with sexual sin in our local churches?
5. Do you believe God cares about your body? Why or why not?

ACTIVITY

Have each person write down an answer to the following question: What does sexual obedience and sexual flourishing look like for you, right now, at this stage of your life? Then have everyone write down a prayer, asking God to help them honor him with their sexuality. If you have time and are willing, break off into groups of two or three and take turns praying each person's prayer for them. Or, share some of your individual prayers with the whole group.

9

WHAT WILL WE TELL OUR CHILDREN?

Jessica grew up in the church during the True Love Waits era. She was told to wear shorts no higher than the length of a dollar bill above her knee, and to avoid mixed bathing and high school dances. If a teenager had sex, "grace was off the table," she said. But at age fifteen, Jessica had sex for first time with a guy from school she'd only just met, in a Super 8 motel, with other friends in the room:

> I had absolutely no identity of my own, and because I got boobs early in life, I was already reduced to believing that's where my commodity and bargaining value was. I had a journal entry from years ago where I wrote down all the things I believed about myself, and it was awful. One of the things said: *Boobs equal Value.* I wasn't taught differently, and the guys around me weren't taught to value bodies, to steward them, to honor the image of God, or that sex is holy. We were told that sex is bad and wrong and sinful, and then BOOM, sex is—not quite a gift—but allowed for married people. I have a friend who spent her wedding night in the ER with a panic attack because she felt so wrong and sinful for starting to do something we had been told for years was wrong.

Jessica's story crushes me. I weep, thinking about my future daughter. My future son. Wondering how I can communicate God's holiness and his grace in equal measure; how I can teach them to live God's sexual ethic without demonizing their God-created bodies and God-given sexuality. I want them to experience joy and peace and excitement and forgiveness. I want to teach them that sex belongs in marriage, without handing them shame like a rite of passage. *Lord, help me. Help us. We want to honor you.*

WHAT WILL WE TELL THEM?

I asked Jessica, "What will you tell your daughter about sexual purity?" This is the question I keep returning to, because we can talk about the freedoms we wish we'd been granted. We can lament the stereotypes we are still trying to disentangle from truth, but when we look at our own children, our true sexual ethic comes out. How we want our children to live, sexually, is what we really believe about sexual purity. When our son hears his older sister crying in her room and asks us what happened on her date, when our daughter discovers her clitoris, when our son has his first wet dream, when our teenager is sexually harassed at school, when we find pornography in their search history, or when they ask us why they can't have sex with their boyfriend or girlfriend—what will we say?

"First, I would teach her who the Father is," Jessica told me, "not just what the rules are. His mercy, his patience, his kindness, his love, and his goodness. We would talk most about the Giver, but also about the goodness of the gifts, in their proper context." She added that she would want to be very intentional about affirming her daughter every chance she got and "would plead with God to make her confident in her place as his daughter." Third, she said that she would try not to respond to her daughter's sins with shock. She would want her daughter to know that she can run toward Jesus when she sins. And she added: "I would tell her my story when she was ready to hear it."

Jackie Hill Perry says that if she could teach her daughter anything about herself, "it would be that because a good God made the woman then *being* a woman [is] a *good* thing."[1] If I ever have a son, I want him to know the same, that God created man and called that creation good. God created them, male and female, and was pleased with the finished product. Whatever our physical insecurities—the things we wish we could change about our bodies—God made us, and he is pleased with his creation.

Our bodies are precious to him. It was not only Jesus' soul pain on the cross that hurt God but the way his flesh was torn by thorns and nails, the way he was stripped, humiliated by public nakedness, and whipped almost to the point of death. Our bodies matter to God. What we do in our bodies matters to God. What others do to our bodies matters to God.

But even if we can convince our children that their hands are beautiful for coloring and writing and playing in the mud, that their feet will carry them to rivers, across basketball courts, and to school, or that their smile can light up a room and their tears are seen by a holy God, there are parts of the body that don't feel as safe, wonderful, or holy.

While happily twirling in church, a little girl is told to put her skirt down so that her underwear is not on display. When a little boy goes outside to play, he is told that he must wear pants. We learn early on that certain parts of our body are to be kept hidden. We learn what modesty means in our cultural context. We learn about privacy and private parts. The mystery piques our curiosity. What is so special, we wonder, about this part or that part, that it must be kept hidden? Sometimes we are chastised for asking, for looking, or for wondering. Nakedness and curiosity, which were adorable in our early years, become a source of embarrassment. And our bodies absorb the shame.

It was not always this way. It was not until sin entered the world that Adam and Eve felt the need to hide their nakedness. And we too understand that our nakedness is not safe in a world filled with sin and selfishness. We do not live in the Garden of Eden. Our bodies, created good, have been used for evil. They have been abused. Our bodies, still good, are both what we use to bless others and also what we use to sin against them, against ourselves, and against a holy God.

In the Old Testament, the basic functions and responses of the human body pose a threat to the holiness of God's house. In Moses' law, if someone carries disease, touches a dead body, or produces bodily fluid, they are considered ritually unclean for days and must wash themselves thoroughly before entering the temple. But Jesus changed all that. He lived holy, died obediently, and rose in purity and power. Jesus is the only reason we can talk to God whenever we want. He tore the temple curtain in half. Whatever our state, we can boldly approach the throne of God because of Jesus Christ. In him, we have been made pure.

But embodiment, post-Eden, is complicated. The days of happily wading in the kiddy pool, naked and carefree, are short-lived. Before our children start feeling the need to grab fig leaves to cover up, we have an opportunity. It begins with something as simple as the words we use. Do we talk about the human body with shame or joy? Do we use the right terms, or do we add embarrassment to certain body parts by veiling them in euphemisms? Each parent, of course, has to decide for themselves what is best. I don't have children yet, and I imagine it would feel a bit strange to use words like *penis* or *vagina* with a small child. But part of the reason it would feel awkward is because I have it in my head that these are "mature" words, words they shouldn't know until they get older. I think it's important to ask myself why I feel this way.

One of the main reasons is that these words were not used in my family when I was growing up. We went with the classic *peepee* and *weenie* in my house (and some other, less traditional words too, but I will spare you those; feel free to pause here for a moment and chuckle over the embarrassing euphemisms your family came up with—we all had them). Our families weren't wrong. If you use silly names with your children, you are not wrong. This isn't a moral issue, and I have no desire to cause anyone false guilt over it. But I will suggest a few reasons why using anatomically correct terminology with your children could be a positive thing, thinking ahead to their view of their own bodies and sexuality.

One woman I interviewed explained to me why she has chosen to use anatomically correct terms with her children: "If I am laying the groundwork that even the language we use is okay, then when my daughter starts to have physical reactions—if she discovers that something hurts, or that something is pleasurable, she can come to me and ask: 'Hey, what is happening in my body?' And I can use the language she is already familiar with." My friend Holly added that, as a nurse, using the correct terminology helps her when "telling kids about their bodies and what God designed each organ for."

"If, God forbid, something sexual is done to my child," one mom shared, "the only term that the law will accept is the anatomically correct one." And this is the other reason. Using the right terms gives children the language to recognize and report sexual abuse. Thinking back to Abby Perry's interview with Ruthy Nordgren, it stands out to me that Ruthy shared, "I didn't understand molestation or rape. Not understanding made it possible for it to continue and turn into far worse."[2] While we may consider certain subjects or even words too mature for our young children, acknowledging these truths and the right terminology empowers them to report sexual abuse and to understand what is and isn't appropriate as far as physical touch from others. I hate that sexual abuse exists. I also hate that young children too often do not have the words or understanding to seek help.

Joy Beth Smith puts it this way: "I'm not ashamed of having a nose. It's simply part of my body, and I learned its name early. No one insisted I call it a smelly-smelly. In using nicknames, we infantilize our own anatomy, further perpetuating the culture of silence around sex—and sexual abuse."[3] And we further increase unnecessary humiliation over body parts that are not inherently sinful. It may seem like a small thing, but one step toward removing shame around our God-given sexuality is to talk to our children in clear, correct terminology about their bodies.

(RE)DEFINING SEXUALITY

"It is not wrong to be a sexual person," Rebecca Lemke writes.[4] For some, this statement might give pause. The terms *sexuality* and *sex* are so often entangled in our minds, it can be hard to distinguish between the two. In her book *Pure,* Klein says: "most evangelical youth are a lot like I was in the years after I left the church—sexual, and ashamed of it."[5] It is not only sexual actions or sinful lust but the state of being a sexual person that causes shame for so many in the church. How can we talk to our children about what sexuality means?

Debra Hirsch is such a source of wisdom here. She points out that for too long sexuality has been viewed as "a dangerous paganizing force in our souls and in society" —something "unredeemed and unredeemable."[6] But is this how Christians should view sexuality? Nancy Pearcey believes that thinking about sexuality as synonymous with sexual hedonism is a "bleak, one dimensional view" that assumes "that sex is just a physical urge—that there is no deeper, more holistic yearning to connect with another person."[7]

Not only is there a difference between sexuality and sex, there is also a difference between sexuality and sexual sin. Our children need to understand this distinction. They need to understand that their desire to be wanted and loved, to experience sexual intimacy, or the physical fact that their bodies experience sexual arousal, is not sinful. To be sure, these God-given desires can quickly become distorted by our sin and selfishness, but the state of being a sexual person is not sinful. More than that, it is *good*.

Are we preparing our children to expect their sexuality, or to be surprised and embarrassed by it? Do we only talk about sexuality in terms of sexual sin, or do we also talk about it as a God-created good? Perhaps we think that silence on the subject is safest. The sad truth is that many of my peers inherited more sexual shame from what was *not* said than what was said. Silence left room for secrecy, misinterpretation, and feelings of alienation. Surely if a subject was too embarrassing to talk about out loud, it was sinful to feel or be curious about.

The more our children are taught to fear sexuality, the more—not less—likely they are to struggle with sexual sin. Shame pushes people into dark corners, where sin breeds. Many of the women I interviewed admitted to me that their pornography addictions began as internet searches, born from a curiosity to understand things that seemed too embarrassing to discuss out loud, things they were ashamed to be feeling or curious about. If our children are, instead, equipped with an understanding that sexuality is universal and good, they are more likely to step out into the light with their experiences, questions, and struggles. If they know that to be human is to be sexual, then maybe—just maybe—when sexual temptation comes their way, they will feel less alone and more willing to ask for help.

Hirsch points out that our sexuality is more than just who we're attracted to, our sexual organs, or the act of sex itself.[8] She says, "Sexuality can be described as the deep desire and longing that drives us beyond ourselves in an attempt to connect with, to understand, that which is other than ourselves. Essentially, it is a longing to know and be known by other people (on physical, emotional, psychological, and spiritual levels). It thus forms part of what it means to 'love others as we love ourselves' (Mark 12:29-31)."[9] This summary of sexuality is fuller and more reflective of the *imago Dei* than any other definition I've heard. God created us in his image and we are all sexual beings, which means that being sexual has something to do with how we image God. And while the desire to know and be known is certainly expressed in marriage and sex, if Hirsch is right, it can also be expressed through friendship and our church community.

Romance is not the only avenue to intimacy. By God's grace, he has given us the body of Christ, the church. We may be single, widowed, or divorced, but the church is a place to carry our loneliness and desire for connection. We can sing beside one another, confide in our small group, have dinner together, and carry one another's burdens.

THE IMPORTANCE OF FRIENDSHIP

In an episode of the television show *New Girl*, Nick discovers a lump on his neck. He needs an ultrasound to find out if it's cancerous or not, but he is scared and doesn't have any health insurance. His friends push him to get the ultrasound, drive him there, and when he gets done with the appointment, they are all standing there waiting for him. He fumbles through his wallet, trying to find enough change to pay for the examination, when the receptionist stops him to let him know that the bill has already been covered. He looks at his friends, and they smile back at him, explaining that they combined their money to cover his bill.

There is a reason so much of our favorite fiction revolves around friendship. I remember reading the stories of Betsy, Tacy, and Tib by Maud Hart Lovelace as a child, then The Baby-sitter's Club series as an adolescent, and watching shows like *Cheers*, *Seinfeld*, and *Friends* as a young adult. There was such comfort in the idea of a makeshift family of peers, people you could laugh with and lean on. Sure, some of the characters fell in love with one another, some broke up, while others got married. But there was a closeness there that so many of us longed for.

My friends have been God's grace to me in every season of my life—whether I was dating, married, or single—or divorced, single, or remarried, for that matter. *Every* season. Friendship is so important in all our lives, and we don't talk about it enough. Instead, Christian bookstores, summer camps, and youth groups harp on the topic of sexual purity, which pigeon-holes intimacy as something that can only be found in one relationship and one act. Thank goodness for my parents, who encouraged me to pursue friendships in my early years.

Dating has value but a narrower purpose: enjoying romance, learning how to navigate romantic relationships, or looking for a potential spouse (depending on the individual's goal). But friendship isn't dependent on romantic feelings. It is about living life with others and being there for them. Friendship is about the good and the bad days. The no-makeup days and the boring days. The day when his dad died suddenly from a blood clot. The day she lost her baby. The day he dropped out of school. It's about being there for someone, regardless of how attractive they are or what else you have going on. In friendship, the focus isn't on image, or impressing the other person, or the potential of getting a kiss, but on being present.

By all means, go on dates. But do not fall for the purity culture lie that dating, courting, or marriage have cornered the market on intimacy. Our view of intimacy is too narrow, too entangled with the act of sex itself, when we think that it can only be achieved inside a dating or married relationship. This distorted thinking makes cross-gender friendships seem like a threat to purity instead of precious gifts from God. And it leaves little room for the kind of intimacy we see in the early church, like in Romans 16, when Paul talks about his brothers and sisters with so much love and familiarity: sister Phoebe, bold Priscilla and Aquila, beloved Epaenetus, hardworking Mary, forerunners of the gospel Andronicus and Junia, and so on. Paul loves these saints like his family. He appreciates them, he *knows* them, and he affirms them without hesitation.

When marriage and sex become the goal of our lives, we can easily miss out on the intimacy of kinship and the joy of friendship in the church. One of my friends who is same-sex attracted and celibate told me that she believes we must work harder to see one another "with the eyes of God toward his image in them," because this "is the most powerful tool against objectification we have." Instead of hyperfocusing on the problem of lust, maybe we should start by talking about the value of our siblinghood in Christ and our shared identity as image bearers of God.[10]

We lose a great gift when we neglect cross-gender friendship. A woman I interviewed shared a story with me about her time at Bob Jones University, where physical contact between men and women was absolutely prohibited, aside from graduation day when hugs were allowed, and during Christmas chapel, when students held hands while singing a Christmas song. One day, before class started, her friend pulled her aside and told her that he had just gotten a call that his father had committed suicide. He wouldn't be returning to school. As hundreds of students walked by, she listened to his grief with her hands at her sides. She wanted to hug him, to comfort him, but she didn't. "There was nothing sexual about it, but we both knew that we couldn't do anything or we'd get in trouble," she said.

This is the loss we incur by oversexualizing cross-gender friendships and by fixating on lust instead of promoting familial intimacy. For believers, there is a place made just for this kind of love: the church. Sam Allberry says that just because a relationship is "non-sexual and also non-romantic doesn't mean it lacks healthy biblical intimacy." He continues: "Scripture shows us that such friendships don't need exclusivity or improper physicality in order to become genuine and deep. Jesus testifies to this in how he describes his disciples as his friends (John 15:15)."[11]

PRESS INTO THE CHURCH

The church is our home: a refuge for the lonely, the hurting, the tired new mother, the widowed father, the single and celibate. It should be a place where we can be honest about our longings, frustrations, and sins. Many of us are weary from fighting the flesh, and we are made wearier when we try to do it alone. Winner points out that "though we are willing to talk about sex from the pulpit, we are often less comfortable initiating hard conversations with our brothers and sisters about sex in people's real day-to-day lives."[12] I know it's awkward. I know we are only used to talking about sex and sexuality in certain contexts and in certain ways. But reading a book or article, as helpful as it may be, is different than having someone in your local body know your struggles. Because they will ask you about it. They will pray for you. They will look at you and *know.* It is a terrifying, vulnerable thing.

I am just as uncomfortable with this idea as you are. I would like to keep my most personal struggles a secret from those who see me on a regular basis. Being known is terrifying. But one of the greatest gifts we can give our children is to live in humble vulnerability in our churches. They should see us drawing close to our brothers and sisters in Christ in love and purity. We can model for them what intimacy within the body looks like. We can lead the way.

Sometimes this will look like confessing our struggles out loud in a small group, or asking for prayer for something that's hard to admit. It will look like seeking wisdom from the body before making important decisions. It will mean having church members into our homes, eating, drinking, and laughing together, celebrating together, and grieving together. When our children see that love and intimacy are not only found in marriage but also in the church, they'll know that there is always a place for them to go with their loneliness and longings.

SEXUAL EXPRESSION

It's clear that we need a whole-person theology when it comes to sexual expression. "Christ did not die to redeem us in part," Perry says, "neither did He rise so that we might have life in portions."[13] In other words, the pursuit of holiness involves the soul *and* the body. The two are connected. What we do in the body matters to God. What Jesus did in his body mattered—so much that we now have access to eternal life through his physical death and physical resurrection. A right view of the *imago Dei* means that we look at ourselves and others this way: as a body *and* a soul, made in the image of the holy God. This is where our conversations about sexual purity must always begin.

Hooking up. I recently scanned the "Sex and Relationships" section of *Teen Vogue* to see what was happening in the cultural conversation surrounding sexuality for teens. Just a few minutes of scrolling lead me to the following article titles: "How to Get an Abortion If You Don't Want to Tell Your

Parents"; "Queer Sex 101: How to Have Sex and Do it Safely"; "What to Say—and Not Say—When Your Friend Tells You They Have Herpes"; "How to Sext—Safely."[14]

Sexual ethics in America today have been largely reduced to a matter of safety and consent. And while sexual expression should never be about *less* than safety and consent, for Christians it has to be about more. Pearcey discovered in her research that modern hookup culture centers around the skill of separating what one does with their body from what they do with their emotions. The typical rules of hookup culture are to avoid emotional attachment, relationship, commitment, and exclusivity. "The script is that you are supposed to be able to walk away from the experience as if it did not happen," Pearcey concludes.[15] Enjoying multiple sexual partners without getting emotionally entangled means learning how to separate what you do with your body from what you do with your heart.

What a contrast to God's design for sex within marriage! Married sex takes place in the context of commitment. It says to another person, "You can trust me with your body, your heart, and your life because I am pledged to you. We are one." It often involves pleasure, but it is *about* faithfulness, unity, and service. It is about being there for them before and after sex, when they get home from work, when they're sick with the flu, struggling with depression, or unsure of where they belong.

By God's design, sex also introduces the potential of children. While procreation is not always possible, nor is it a requirement in marriage, children are a tangible illustration of the unifying nature of sex. Sex is *meant* to tether two people together. Even without children, trying to disconnect sex from commitment and emotions is biologically difficult because, as Pearcey points out, sex is known to produce attachment hormones like oxytocin and vasopressin.[16] While hookup culture attempts to reduce sex to a mere exchange of consent and sexual fluids, God invented sex to bond two people together.

Pornography. Barna surveyed almost three thousand Americans, both adolescents and adults, in a study that came out in 2016. Young adults rated failing to recycle and the overconsumption of water and electricity as more immoral than viewing pornography.[17] While it is encouraging that this upcoming generation cares about the environment, it is deeply troubling to see such cavalier attitudes toward pornography.

However, it isn't surprising. Have you watched any sitcoms recently? Characters talk about pornography with a chuckle, as though it's not only something everyone does but something we need no longer blush at. In an episode of the show *Friends*, which began in the late 1990s, Chandler quickly changes the channel when his girlfriend walks into the room so that she won't catch him watching porn. But in a recent episode of *New Girl,* which began in 2011, a group of friends watches pornography together on their living room couch. One character complains, but it's a lighthearted, humorous scene.

But even in secular culture there are those waking up to the fact that pornography is not an innocent pastime. Actor Russell Brand, who believes that sex should be about intimacy and mutual consent, has lately been speaking out against pornography. In a video on his YouTube channel, Brand admits that he has been awash with pornography since he was young and has struggled to give it up entirely. He says it has made objectifying women easier. For example, instead of wondering about what a woman is like "as a soul, as another person," he says that, too often, he dwells solely on her body. He hates this and urges others to look at the research coming out about the damaging impact of pornography on our brains and relationships with others.[18] Viewing pornography "literally changes the chemistry of our brains."[19] In pornography, you can own someone in your mind, sexually, without their permission, and without caring about them as a human being or image bearer of God. Pornography reduces our neighbor, who we are called to love, to a sexual object.

"You have a crush on a girl? With a little bit of persuasion, you can convince her to send you a topless photo. You get to experience her body—and probably personal pleasure—without intimacy, without physical proximity, without any of the embodied risks of physical sex. You give nothing of yourself," says Roxanne Stone with Barna research regarding teenagers and "Porn 2.0." Barna's research shows that 62 percent of adolescents and young adults admitted to having received "a nude image from someone else via text, email, social media or app" and 40 percent said they have sent a nude image at some point.[20]

Stone points out that the younger generation has a "morality of self-fulfillment," viewing good and evil in relation to its societal impact. "Watching pornography," she says, is viewed by adolescents as an "individual choice. Affecting no one but me." But we do not understand pornography if we think it's a victimless industry, or that viewing it doesn't hurt anyone. It has been proven over and over again that "porn fuels the demand for sex trafficking."[21] It has also been proven that it hurts our relationships with one another, sexually and otherwise.

And we have misunderstood what sexual purity means if we think that viewing pornography is an innocent expression of our sexuality. Twitter polls can only tell us so much, as they show us sample size but not demographics, but I decided to ask this question: Have you ever viewed pornography as a way to satiate sexual desire so as to avoid the temptation to have premarital sex? 141 people responded and 22 percent admitted that they have viewed pornography for this purpose.[22] Pornography may seem like a loophole when it comes to satiating sexual desire outside of marriage, but sexual purity is not achieved by finding ways to hide or isolate lust.

Samuel L. Perry notes that the rise in pornography usage is not only due to society's acceptance of it but its "accessibility" and "anonymity."[23] It is one of the easiest sexual sins to hide, and according to Perry's research, Protestants are "losing the battle with pornography," not so much in regard to exposure to pornography but addiction to it.[24] With such an emphasis on virginity and *appearing* pure, purity culture rhetoric may have pushed some Christians into deeper hiding when it comes to the use of pornography. Sin breeds in the darkness, and sadly pornography is something we can look at, on our phones or laptops, in secret.

"We are naturally curious about sexuality," one parent told me, explaining that her approach is to ask her children about pornography so that she can help them, not punish them. She tells her children that "Satan is a liar and sin is a liar. And our thoughts and hearts and sins will start to tell us 'No one else will understand. You can't get back from this.' But the message of Jesus is always 'it is safe in the light.' We have to tell kids that they will be safe in the light."

It is safe for you to come into the light as well. While there is an undeniably casual attitude toward the use of pornography in our culture today, I noticed a very different attitude throughout my interviews. The Christians I spoke with did not try to excuse their behavior. Rather, it was clear that their struggle with pornography was a huge source of shame —especially for women who had the added layer of embarrassment over struggling with a so-called man's sin. A few admitted that their shame has created a cycle of sin, where the more ashamed they become, the deeper they delve into pornography as a coping mechanism. We are not loving the church or our neighbor if we think shame is the solution. We must give our brothers and sisters permission to step into the light of transparency and forgiveness. We must put our arms around them and tell them that they don't have to fight this sin alone.

Masturbation. Jude Law plays Gigolo Joe in Steven Spielberg's 2001 film *A.I.: Artificial Intelligence*. Joe is a robotic male prostitute who tells his customer: "Patricia, once you've had a lover robot, you'll never want a real man again."[25] Similarly, masturbation gives us the ability to achieve orgasm without any communication or vulnerability with another human being. You can take what you want, how you want it, whenever you want. It reminds me of Burger King's old slogan: "Have it your way." In both its convenience and the feelings of regret Christians often feel afterward, masturbation is the fast food of sex.

In this section I will be talking about masturbation in terms of the private, solo act—not something mutually agreed on and performed inside marriage. If there is one struggle that came up over and over again in my interviews, it was solo sex. Even though it is seldom talked about, masturbation is one of the most common sexual struggles for Christians, both for singles and marrieds. And one of the struggles surrounding masturbation is the silence of Scripture on the subject. Not only are we hush-hush about it in our Christian circles, it is also difficult to find any passages in the Bible that address it.

What is debatable is whether or not masturbation is always accompanied by sinful lust. For example, it is quite common—though rarely discussed—for toddlers to discover masturbation as a source of self-comfort and enjoyment.[26] Some married couples who are forced to spend a great deal of time apart might agree to use individual masturbation, with their spouse in mind, as a way to connect with one another long distance. And I know Christians who view masturbation as a gift to be practiced with self-control, the same way one might indulge in a piece of cheesecake or a glass of red wine. Others see it as black and white, believing that masturbation is always a sin, no matter the circumstance or motivation. I believe that we can, in good faith, land in different places on this issue.

But I will share my perspective, as if we were all sitting together at a Bible study, with our notebooks, coffee cups, and pens scattered around—and I hope your thinking about the subject will not end with my words. I believe that while masturbation might not be a sin in every circumstance, it deserves to be questioned. Like all our practices, we need to ask ourselves if it brings glory to God. Can we masturbate and honor God at the same time? Does masturbating align with God's design for sex? Does it help us love our neighbor? Do masturbation and lust go together for us? How we answer these questions will reveal our motives, goals, and heart before God.

Our hearts often deceive us, especially when we want something badly enough. If you have masturbated, you've probably gone through a list of justifications that sound something like this: "I just needed help falling asleep," "I needed to get it out of my system," "I didn't want to bother my spouse," "I was lonely," "It was too late at night to text my accountability partner," "I was listening to my body," or "It doesn't hurt anyone." And brother or sister, I hear you. You are not alone. The struggle is real.

One woman I interviewed shared that masturbation was something she used to cope when growing up in an abusive home. "It was one way I could have control; a way I could connect with myself." For some married couples, masturbation may seem quicker and easier than asking their spouse for sex. Some use masturbation as a form of stress relief, while others use it to deal with their lust, hoping to shorten the struggle. Many have become addicted. Winner points out that "God's creation, including human bodies, is good, but it does not follow that everything bodies do is good."[27] Our ability to achieve orgasm is a God-created miracle, but does this mean that we have the right to seek it out whenever we want?

I believe that solo sex says to God, "You are not giving me something I need, so I'm going to take it." And this attitude is so hard to keep from spreading like a cancer. Not just in the act of masturbation, which quickly becomes addictive, but in other areas of our lives. Eve Tushnet argues that instead of allowing celibacy to drive us "to pour ourselves out for others" or accepting "all the hard, weird, disappointing realities of sex and marriage," masturbation teaches us to view our sexuality selfishly.[28] Masturbation is something we do by ourselves, with ourselves, and for ourselves. Instead of taking our loneliness and unmet longings to God in prayer, we seek only our own relief. Instead of giving our spouse the opportunity to know us and serve us, we forsake grace and do it ourselves. Instead of benefitting from the lessons we might learn from self-denial and self-discipline, we take what we want, when we want it.

In the same way we need to walk in the light of fellowship with struggles like pornography, we don't have to wrestle with masturbation alone. The place to start is to talk to God about it. Tell him everything and ask him to convict you rightly. Then bring it into the light of fellowship by confiding in a trusted friend, mentor, or small group. If you are convicted that masturbation is a sin for you, here are practical ways to resist the temptation, whether you are married, single, widowed, same-sex attracted, or whatever your situation.

- Train yourself to respond to the temptation by finding a place where you cannot masturbate (for example, take a walk outside).
- Tell God about it. Tell God how frustrated you are to want something so much and not being able to satisfy it. Pour out your longings, disappointments, and ask him to help

you through this trial—whether it lasts five minutes or much longer.

- Take preemptive action by considering your entertainment habits. Are you watching movies, videos, and TV shows that increase your temptation to masturbate? Cut that entertainment out of your life temporarily or permanently, as wisdom dictates.
- Replace lies with truth. Do you have the power to say no? Yes. Will it be difficult? Yes.
- Find someone you trust to confide in about this struggle. As them to ask you about it periodically. Be honest with them. Ask for prayer when the temptation arises.

Whatever you think about this issue, be willing to ask yourself these questions. It is good for our souls to wrestle with these things in light of God's commands, his love, and his mercy. Ultimately, I hope you know that there is forgiveness at the cross. There is no limit to what God, in Jesus, can forgive. If you fell off the wagon, it doesn't mean you can't start fresh today. And if you fall again today, it doesn't mean you can't start fresh tomorrow. His mercies are new every morning. Great is his faithfulness.

HOW FAR IS TOO FAR?

I am not the first person, nor should I be the last, to point out that asking "how far is too far?" in regard to sexual expression is probably not the right question. Regardless, it is the question our children *will* ask because they are human and it is reasonable to wonder how much and what kind of physical affection they can show outside of marriage. It's not an easy question to answer, is it?

Too many of the Christian authors I read as an adolescent tried to answer this question with a list of rules that all Christian teenagers were supposed to follow such as: don't date until you're ready for marriage; save your first kiss for the altar; if you're going to kiss, don't do it horizontally; never be alone together in a car; never be alone together period; don't pray together—spiritual intimacy leads to physical intimacy; always pray together—prayer keeps lust at bay.

You may notice that some of the rules contradict each other. It was a choose-your-own-adventure situation—whichever book was "trending" in your youth group or church at the time—that was usually the purity standard for all. In my home church, there were a few different books making the rounds, so we had families who would only let their children "court"—where parental involvement was key—while others were reading books by Eric and Leslie Ludy, Elisabeth Elliot, and Joshua Harris, so they thought dating was permissible but serious—meant only for the purpose of finding a spouse. You could kiss and cuddle but only if you thought you were going to marry that person.

The impression we got from these books, whether the authors intended it or not, was that if we followed the rules exactly, we would succeed in sexual purity. The possibility that there may never be a wedding day wasn't even a footnote, and the same-sex attracted and those harmed by sexual abuse were rarely, if ever, acknowledged. While these authors had a noble goal and some wisdom to offer, gray areas were painted black and white. Instead of being encouraged to develop individual discernment and face our own personal struggles with lust head on, many of us followed the rules laid out for us and learned how to *look* pure without actually practicing purity.

When I was a high school teacher, I watched how my students found ways to technically follow the school dress code while still expressing low-key rebellion. They would wear crazy socks under their slacks or huge bows in their hair. One day, a girl showed up with zombie eyes because she had put in fake contacts. My point is: we find loopholes. The young woman wearing long skirts and saying no to dates might also be maintaining a very active sexual imagination. The young man who boasts about saving his first kiss for his fiancée might also be looking at pornography on his phone at night. Sometimes lists of extrabiblical rules actually give us the opportunity to look and feel spiritual when we are really living in unrepentant sin.

I remember hearing about an evangelical megachurch in Southern California that decided to put a note in their church bulletin asking female congregants to refrain from wearing shirts and dresses with spaghetti straps to church. Abby Perry gives us some insight into the kind of logic behind decisions like this: "If boys saw bra straps, they'd think about bras. If they thought about bras, they'd think about breasts. If they thought about breasts, they'd be tempted to lust, and that would be our fault."[29] This thinking says: rules are the solution. Rules about modesty, rules about dating, rules about kissing. Lust is solvable if Christians would only follow the rules.

Beloved, our hearts don't work this way. If we want to sin, we will find a way. If lust is our goal, we will meet that goal, inside or outside the rules. In a world where pornography is just a few clicks away and the media constantly promotes sexual exploration, the temptation to sexual sin meets us at every turn. It is not hard to find ways to sin sexually. Asking the women at your church to cover more of their shoulders is not the solution to sexual impurity when the billboard on the way to church features a woman's cleavage and the strip club down the street is lit up like a Christmas tree.

This doesn't mean that rules are wrong. Parents and institutions must have them. But if our desire is to teach our children how to live truly holy lives from the heart, we must understand the limits of our lists. If our desire is that they continue in purity long after leaving our care, we must teach them discernment, honesty, and how to search their own hearts. Legalism creeps in when we put our human rules about hugging and kissing on the same level of authority as Scripture. And lazy spirituality results when we teach our children that following our rules is all it takes to honor God.

Our children can make it to their wedding day as virgins and still be caught up in sexual sin. In encouraging virginity, we must also be honest about this: that appearing pure isn't the same thing as pursuing sexual purity. We can fool ourselves, but we can't fool God. I wish someone had told me how much sexual purity has to do with being honest with yourself. Because, though I have always been good at following rules, I have often fallen short of God's sexual ethic.

I got the chance to think through purity culture rules versus personal discernment when I dated the second time around, after my divorce. Having been married before, I knew more about what was sexually tempting for me and what wasn't. I knew what my boundaries needed to be. If you talk to your friends about their individual temptations to lust, you might be surprised at where some of them draw the line and others don't. There are certain things we can probably all agree invite sexual temptation, but other things really depend on the individual. It's important to remind our children that in dating it is not only their unique temptations to sexual lust that matter but their partner's also. While they might be able to kiss passionately without being tempted to have sex, the person they are dating might find this difficult and discouraging to their pursuit of purity.

When it comes to holiness in sexual expression, we must first look to God and his Word. There are clear guidelines there: sex is for marriage between one man and one woman. Outside of that, we must ask ourselves if we are loving him with all our heart, soul, mind, and body and loving our neighbor as ourselves with our sexuality. Asking this question provides us with a pause before action. It is in this pause that we create space to consider our motivations, our neighbor, and God's glory. I often pray, *God, give me that moment of pause, to recognize temptation to sin when it is happening. Then, give me the power, through your Holy Spirit, to do the right thing.*

HOW TO TALK TO TEENAGERS ABOUT SEXUALITY

If you are a parent, you might be skimming this book for practical advice. I get that. As you have no doubt gathered, I don't believe there is a universal set of extrabiblical rules that we should be handing every teenager, assuring them and ourselves that following them will guarantee sexual purity. I will leave your house rules up to you, but here I want to offer some practical advice about how to go about initiating conversations about sexuality with your teenagers.

I should state that I am not a parent yet. I hope you will find my advice helpful anyway, as it is drawn from years of working with teenagers and a decade spent teaching high school students. During lunch I would open up my classroom doors and invite my female students to eat with me. We usually talked about their friends, future plans, and the TV shows they were watching, but sometimes they wanted to tell me about who they had a crush on, their fears about dating, and even about their childhood sexual abuse, their addiction to pornography, or their regrets over going "too far" with a guy. It was incredible to me what they would share during a twenty-minute lunch break, under iridescent lights and over mediocre sandwiches.

Be a listener. Maybe you already feel like you're a good listener. In fact, you would like to listen *more,* if only your son or daughter would let you in. But a good listener is not just someone who invites conversation. Good listening has to do with how you respond after they share their heart with you. If your teenager tells you about a problem they are having, you are probably going to want to respond with advice and offers to help. This is natural and loving. Of course we want to help! We don't like to see anyone, especially our children, struggle.

But this is often where we lose them. They wanted to be heard. They wanted to feel safe enough to say something out loud. Just sharing took all the courage they could muster, and now they just need to know that you still love them. Often the best thing we can do after someone shares their heart with us is to thank them. Pause and affirm their bravery. Then, remind them that no matter what they are struggling with, have done, or have had done to them, you love them and always will.

Being a good listener doesn't mean that you never give advice, guide, or correct your children. And of course, if they are in trouble, it is absolutely your job to protect them and report any abuse to the proper authorities. But when it is not a case of abuse, when your teenager is confiding in you about their struggle with masturbation, their attraction to people of their own gender, or what they did with their boyfriend last night, you have to be willing to allow for some silence, some space in between their vulnerability and your plan of action. First Thessalonians 5:14 says: "And we urge you, brothers, admonish the idle, encourage the fainthearted, help the weak, be patient with them all" (ESV). Our children don't always need us to tell them what to do. Sometimes, they just need us to be present and listen.

Avoid expressing shock. I am a very expressive person. People often tell me that I can't hide what I'm feeling because I wear it on my face. The first time one of my students told me what had happened to them as a child, how they had been sexually abused, it was everything I could do not to burst into tears in the middle of their sentence. It's not that weeping over someone else's pain is wrong—in fact, sometimes this is exactly what Scripture calls us to do. But I was being asked to listen to someone's story, and I knew that they wouldn't continue if they felt their pain was hurting me.

When teenagers ask certain questions, it can stop our hearts and cause our minds to race about why they might be asking that particular question. This is probably one of the reasons they seldom ask their sexual questions out loud. They are worried about how it will come across. They are embarrassed by their curiosity or lack of knowledge. If we can do our best to hold our shock at bay and hear them out, I believe the teenagers in our lives will feel more encouraged to share with us.

One of my favorite college literature professors used to say, "As Christians, sin should always offend us, but it should never shock us." I think our children need to know that we will always guide them to God's Word and his standard but that their sin doesn't shock us. That we believe the Bible when it says that each of us sin and fall short of the glory of God. When our children fail in purity, we will be disappointed. We will be grieved. But what they need to know more than anything is that we love them, and that God does too—that he is gracious and merciful, slow to anger, and quick to forgive.

Utilize their entertainment habits. One way I would engage my students was by using what they were already watching, reading, and listening to as a jumping-off point. I didn't like that my eighth graders were watching the sitcom *How I Met Your Mother*, a show about a group of thirty-year-olds who talk openly about sleeping around and watching pornography, but I overheard them talk about the show and decided to use it one day as a chance to talk about biblical sexuality. I asked, "So, how do you feel about the way sex is portrayed in that show?" And a conversation ensued.

Another time I heard a male student singing a song with lyrics that objectified women. I'd heard it on the radio the day before. I asked him, "What do you think about the way that song portrays women?" This brought up other similar songs and movies, and ultimately resulted in a conversation about how we need to view one another as image bearers rather than sexual objects.

Did something happen in the news recently? Have you overheard your kids talking about a certain movie? Use what they are already interested in to start a conversation about how sexuality is depicted, what they think about it, and how God's Word would speak to that issue.

Don't make sex an idol or a dirty word. As Christians talking about sex, we tend to fall into one of two traps: we either demonize it or idolize it. Sex is not a dirty word. But when we talk more about the ways sex has been perverted and distorted than the God-created good of sexuality, we risk vilifying it. On the other hand, sex is not God. Within marriage, it is a gift, but it is not to be worshiped. It is only a shadow, not glory. In her book *Things Your Mother Never Told You,* Kim Gaines Eckert observes that:

> We have begun worshipping the creation, sex, rather than the Creator God (Romans 1:25) . . . but neither our identity as sexual beings, nor the gift of sexual pleasure, is the thing itself. God has created us for union with himself, and sex and sexuality are signs that point us toward that ultimate good. Sex is wonderful, but it is not the ultimate. When we mistake it for such, we are bound to be disappointed.[30]

Somehow—and the balance is difficult to strike—we need to help adolescents understand that their sexuality is good but also that expressing it in a God-honoring, neighbor-loving way will be difficult. Viewing our bodies, sex, and marriage biblically is a lifelong challenge, one that takes work, active obedience, and leaning into the body of Christ. The fight is worth it, regardless of what we suffer or gain, because God's glory is worth it.

If you let teenagers talk honestly with you, you'll end up weeping with them over sexual abuse and their shame over sexual sins. You'll find yourself getting to encourage them as they fight addictions to pornography, habitual masturbation, and lust. You will get to pray over them and love them as they question their sexual identity, the goodness of their bodies, and whether or not it is really worth it to lay down their lives in order to pick up the cross of Christ. It won't be easy, but God will be with you.

DISCUSSION QUESTIONS

1. If you ever have children, what will you tell them about sexuality and sexual purity? Or, if your children are older, what *did* you tell them? Would you do it differently now?
2. What should we tell children about their bodies? What is your opinion about using anatomically correct terminology when talking to young children about their bodies?
3. Can men and women be friends? Why or why not?
4. What would you say to someone who refuses to "press into the church" because they have been hurt by the church?
5. What are some practical things we can do in our local churches to make them a home, a family, and a refuge for those who enter?
6. How do hookup culture, pornography, and masturbation distort God's intended design for sex?

ACTIVITY

Separate into smaller groups and discuss a pop culture artifact (for example, a song, movie, TV show, video game, news story) that could be used as a jumping-off point to start a conversation about sexuality with teenagers. What different topics might this artifact bring up? What guiding questions could you ask? Get back together as one group and discuss what each group came up with.

10

PURITY CULTURE MOVING FORWARD

Community is only as rich and deep as it is diverse. When we limit ourselves to a whole bunch of people who are exactly like us, we're limiting the refining power of community not only to meet needs but also to sanctify. Find friends who look different from you, who work in different areas, who value different things, who are older than you. These voices can speak truth into your life, truth you may have missed.

Joy Beth Smith

Imagine a church where widows and adolescents discuss the struggle of chastity together, where single moms, divorcees, married couples, and the same-sex attracted gather to study the Bible and pray. A place where no prayer request, question, or struggle is taboo or off limits because we have set our makeshift halos aside and admitted our shared humanity. Imagine us holding one another up in our weakest moments instead of wrestling the darkness alone. Imagine a gathering of saints where God's Word is held high, his holiness worshiped, and forgiveness in Christ plays like a record on repeat.

I want to rest my weary bones there. I want to be a part of that church.

Jay Newman grew up in a small town in the mid-nineties. He was an athlete, the son of a Southern Baptist pastor. He also caught the full wave of the True Love Waits movement. "I was the target demographic for Lifeway and Mardels," he told me, chuckling. He would carry his Bible on top of his textbooks as he walked from class to class. To him, the message of True Love Waits made sense. Jay said: "From what I understood, it seemed like a consistent message throughout Scripture that our sexuality was a big deal to God and it was something holy." So he got behind the movement full-heartedly, going so far as to write his own purity pledge and Xerox around five hundred copies, which he then posted on every locker at his school. "It created quite a buzz," he said. "It started a conversation. A lot of people came up to me and said they wanted to sign it—to make a commitment to wait until marriage to have sex."

He was discouraged when just weeks later he overheard the captain of the cheerleading team, who had signed one of the pledge cards, talking about her recent sexual experience. "I just kind of looked at her. I didn't say anything, but in my heart I felt baffled. You signed the card! It was like the commitment didn't mean anything." I asked Jay what he thought about the idea of signing purity pledge cards now. He told me:

> It just became something that you had to do so people would think you're a respectable person. For me, I didn't need to sign a card—it was something I was already about. I was already studying Scripture for myself and had gathered that from my own studies. I didn't need the card. So I don't know who the target was. The people who already felt like sex was a sacred thing and the people who viewed it flippantly continued to view it that way.

Jay and I talked about a lot of things. He pointed out that, because he was a critical thinker, he was able to "eat the fish and spit out the bones," as the saying goes, in regard to purity teachings. He doesn't feel that he was manipulated or lied to by the movement, and he is a proponent of individuals taking ownership over how they listen to and interpret messages. But we agreed that while purity culture has some biblical truth in its spine—mainly, that sex is sacred and meant for marriage—many of its methods and messages have had a harmful effect. Jay admits, "It became kind of like a moral police thing," though he added, "I never felt that was the intent of anyone who ran the program, any of the literature that I read, or anybody who I heard motivating teenagers to participate."

Jay reminds me that purity culture was "just a response to a cultural moment." Our reevaluation of modern purity culture is also a response and as such is susceptible to the same pitfalls, such as overcorrecting and overgeneralizing. I can't tell you how many hours I have spent asking God to give me wisdom as I write this book. Even so, I know that there are things I have said here that will require their own reevaluation, and as a fallible human being, I must welcome that. My greatest hope for this book is that it will spark needed conversations in your homes and local churches, and that those conversations will go beyond what is contained in these pages.

WILLING TO REEVALUATE

Something Joshua Harris said in his recent documentary has stayed with me and echoed over and over again in my head: "You can change your mind about things."[1] This might seem like an obvious statement, but when it comes to our theological beliefs, changing our mind can look like sinking sand. One question could be one step toward drowning. Harris agrees. We spoke on the phone a couple months before he announced his departure from the faith, and he admitted that "once you open the door to being wrong about something, you lose your mojo." He laughed and continued: "Not necessarily, but it can feel like you could be wrong about other things. As a leader or organization in the church, you're always trying to hunker down and protect your position."

As someone who built the majority of his early platform and wealth around one of the most infamous books from modern purity culture, Harris had a lot to lose in questioning his beliefs. But he did it anyway. "I think the truth can handle our questions and God can handle our questions." Harris believes that our hesitation in questioning things is less about our concern that the truth can't withstand it and more about our fear of what people will think. "If you start to ask certain questions, even from the best of motives, you are going to be viewed with suspicion," he said.

Harris noted how difficult this process is, and the raised eyebrows we're likely to encounter along the way. But he received more than just raised eyebrows. Once he began questioning some of his positions in *I Kissed Dating Goodbye* and asking readers how the book had affected them, the floodgates of criticism swung wide open. Those who loved the book were upset that he would amend it in any way, while others aimed all their purity culture baggage directly at him, with full force. But, when I went back and read the most popular books from the modern purity culture era, Harris's was not the greatest offender. I asked him why he had decided to take on blame for all the faults of purity culture, even messages he never promoted. He said,

> I think I felt a sense of responsibility, that, even though my book didn't say a lot of the things that people assume that it says, that it was symbolic of something. And I needed to play the part that I could play in trying to bring healing to people. There is that passage in Jeremiah where God speaks to the unfaithful shepherds and tells them, you didn't bind up, you didn't heal, you didn't care

> for my people, so I'm going to go and do that. I'm going to gather them back and care for them. He's speaking to the religious leaders. And it was a really powerful verse for me right around the time that I was making the decision to go back and do this reevaluation.

He went on to admit that there were moments where he felt defensive and wished he hadn't begun the process. He was almost relieved when the *I Survived I Kissed Dating Goodbye* documentary nearly didn't get fully funded on Kickstarter. Even though he realizes that some people erroneously attribute ideas and quotes to him, he says that it makes sense because his book was "a popularizer, like the gateway drug" to some of the more conservative ideas about dating, modesty, and sexual purity. He admits: "I didn't agree with a lot of the really conservative stuff out there, but my book modernized and popularized it and had the effect of drawing people into ideas that were not helpful." When I asked him if reevaluation is worth it, he said, "Not if you want to stay safe and comfortable."

While writing this book, multiple friends and acquaintances have shared their concern over my questioning something the church has been teaching for so many years. With the recent news of Harris's deconversion, I can see why. Questions have led some, like Harris, to a full-on rejection of the Christian faith. Consequently, questions can look like the beginning of the end. But the idea that asking questions is something only "liberal theologians" do is untrue. Asking questions can be a form of humility when what we are questioning is not God but our own fallible views *about* God. I have built my theological house on the foundation of God's Word. That is not what I am questioning. Rather, I want to examine the influence of Christian subcultures, like purity culture, on our interpretation of God's Word.

My initial response to those pointing out holes in the metaphorical boat of church life is defensiveness. I want to believe that we have grown beyond making mistakes, that I am part of a body that's more fully sanctified. But, beloved, we are a body made up of sinners saved by grace. We mess up. We get things wrong. And we ought to view it as a privilege, not a burden, to do the work of learning how to more clearly and lovingly represent Christ and his Word. But it is hard, humbling work.

Some of you have worked with youth and handed out purity pledge cards. You have taken your teens to purity conferences and passed out copies of *I Kissed Dating Goodbye.* Your desire was to help the young people in your church pursue a life of holiness and to treasure Christ. You understood that sexuality can quickly turn from a good gift into a source of temptation and moral failure. While it is unlikely that any of us, including the authors I mentioned, set out to hurt a generation or preach a false gospel, we must be humble enough to face the damage that has been done. We must be willing to reevaluate our methods and messages against the holy, precious Word of God. This is not the first time, nor should it be the last, that we ask ourselves if we as the church are talking about sexual purity in the right way.

Purity leader Dannah Gresh sat down with Joshua Harris in *I Survived I Kissed Dating Goodbye* and admitted: "I don't think Jesus would do the gum trick," referring to the purity demonstration some youth pastors and conference speakers used where they held up a piece of chewed gum to illustrate what happens to the worth of the sexually impure.[2] We are all in a process of continually evaluating what we say and how it is interpreted. It is difficult work.

Dan Darling points out how it is "always easier to see the blind spots of another culture, and another political position, and another's heart, than it is our own."[3] And so, humility is something we beg God for. Without it, we cannot grow.

STOP TRYING TO MAKE ABSTINENCE SEXY

Perhaps in a good-faith effort to combat secular culture's portrayal of sex as dirty and rebellious, modern purity culture reminded the church that sex is a good thing in marriage. But in order to make married sex worth waiting for, purity rhetoric turned it into a golden calf. Waiting for this idol was only attractive if it was a promise, and "worth the wait." We have a low view of teenagers, young adults, and ourselves if we think that the only way we could possibly motivate someone to follow Christ with their sexuality is by making and believing false promises.

Purity culture's main problem is not that it is too conservative but that it is too worldly. Sex is not about self, and abstinence is anything but sexy. Dressing it up as such is not only confusing, it's discouraging. When our children realize that pursuing sexual purity is incredibly difficult, they will wonder why we didn't prepare them. Sometimes we think God needs us to dangle carrots in front of people in order to make his message palatable, when he has called us to preach a gospel of foolishness to those who are perishing, a message so offensive to our pride that we must either reject the Son or fall at his feet.

There is nothing glamorous or edgy about the pursuit of sexual purity. Have we forgotten that the gate is narrow that leads to life? That we must lay our lives down to pick up our cross and follow Christ? Sex is not a human right, and it is certainly not our Christian right. Some say "love is love," but we know better: *God* is love. We are exiles here. Sojourners. It can be lonely. It *will* be lonely. And yet, Jesus knows all about it. He lived it. We are not alone. As my husband recently said in a sermon, "Jesus created the narrow path for us, with his nail-pierced feet." Jesus himself is with us.

We stumble and fall and tell Jesus with our actions that we think we have found something more satisfying than him. You are not alone in your struggle against the flesh, but beloved, keep struggling *against* it. Make it a tug-of-war. Make it a fight. Do not buy into the theologies that are willing to cut out passages of God's Word to justify their actions or get what they want. God is very clear about where sex belongs: in marriage, between one man and one woman. You will need a sharp pair of scissors to rid your Bible of this truth.

We have become too accustomed to seeking satisfaction for every fleeting desire and long-term want on our own terms. We have begun to believe, along with the world, that this is what freedom means. But true freedom is found in Christ, who forgives all our sins and calls us to walk the narrow road that leads to life, beside him. Jesus obeyed his Father, even to the point of death on a cross. In our struggle against sin we have not yet resisted to the point of shedding our blood (Hebrews 12:4).

Acknowledging that we will sin isn't defeatist. It is an acknowledgment of our humanity. It is preparation to get back up after we fall and try again in his strength. Whatever wagon you are trying desperately not to fall off of, remember: when you fall, and you will, you can dust yourself off and get right back on. God is not counting the days. He is looking for a contrite heart and a humble spirit. Take a moment to repent, to grieve your sin, then open your arms as wide as you can to welcome God's overwhelming grace. His mercies are new every morning.

Lauren Winner defines chastity as an "active undertaking that we do as part of the body . . . not the mere absence of sex but an active conforming of one's body to the arc of the gospel."[4] She says that her pursuit of sexual purity has been aided by the regular means of grace: time in prayer, God's

Word, and his church. "It may sound hokey," Winner says, "but I have prayed regularly that God would reshape my heart and my desires so that I would want the things he wants for me. And every day, I have prayed about sexuality when saying the line from the Lord's Prayer, lead us not into temptation."[5] Not hokey at all. I think sometimes we want a magic formula, a diet plan. But I too have found that nothing has helped me more in my pursuit of sexual purity than talking to God, listening to him in his Word, and spending time with his people. It is not a magic fix but a daily discipline.

ISOLATING PURITY FROM THE GOSPEL

Truly, sexual sin is offensive to God. We commit it against him, our neighbor, and our own bodies. It is something to repent of and seek forgiveness for. But beloved, our sexual failings never negate the purity we have through Jesus Christ. He has washed us white as snow (Isaiah 1:18). You do not have to wait seven days before approaching God after sinning. You do not have to hide outside the camp because "Jesus also suffered outside the city gate to make the people holy through his own blood" (Hebrews 13:12). You have been purchased. You have been pardoned. You are forgiven, beloved, and pure.

We have to start there. If we talk about sexual purity apart from the gospel, we will create chaste Pharisees instead of imperfect disciples. Obedience is a response to grace, not a ladder to heaven. The source of our purity does not come from our own personal striving, goals, or merits. Our pursuit of sexual purity is, rather, a prayer that says: *Thank you, gracious Father, for rescuing me. I will seek to follow you for the rest of my life, in every way, whatever the cost. I will fail. You will forgive. And Your mercies will be new every morning. You are worthy of all praise and glory, forever. Amen.* Every believer is washed permanently and made permanently pure in Christ Jesus. Why wouldn't we thank him for that with our whole lives—including our sexuality?

Winner says that grace was the tutor of chastity in her life, not her "intellectual apprehension of the whys and wherefores of Christian sexual ethics."[6] We can only accomplish so much with lectures and gimmicks. It is grace that speaks louder. We must talk more about the gospel than we do about lust because Christian obedience is about worship. How do we know who and why we worship if the majority of Christian books for adolescents are about dating and chastity rather than the character of God and the worth of Christ? We must get the first things first.

Before you call your teen to chastity, before you talk to the new convert at church, before you examine your own outfit to see if it meets the cultural standards of modesty, remember: the price has already been paid on the cross. Isn't that cause enough to drop our fishing nets, abandon the boat, and follow Christ? He stands ready to save to the uttermost those who are perishing. We need only come to him. The Holy Spirit will comfort and convict, and our desire for obedience, albeit imperfectly lived out, will be our song of praise for the mercy and grace we have received. Our life with God began in grace and will continue in grace.

ONGOING CONVERSATION IN CHRISTIAN COMMUNITY

My friend left me a voicemail recently. "I just heard the youth pastor announce a 'purity weekend' event for the teens at our church," she told me. She wanted to hear my thoughts, knowing I was writing this book.

So here they are. I think isolating the discussion of sexual purity from the rest of Scripture is dangerous. I think we have to ask ourselves: Would we prefer a crowd of teenagers who don't quite understand the gospel but are willing to sign purity pledge cards, or a group of teens who have questions about the Bible and struggle with sexual sin but want to hear more about Jesus? Do we want them to grow into adults who successfully avoided teen pregnancy and STDs but know nothing of the love of Christ, or do we want them to be those who are imperfect, sexually and otherwise, but have a thirst for the things of God? Of course, it is not actually an either-or, but I think it's worth asking the question.

Because if what motivates our purity talks is a desire to keep teenagers from premarital sex, regardless of their eternal state, then we don't understand the nature of eternity. If our desire to get our daughter to the altar a virgin is greater than our desire to see her truly accept Jesus as her Savior, we don't understand the glorious riches of Christ. Purity is important to God—so important that Jesus, the spotless Lamb of God, had to die so that we could live. But, too often, purity rhetoric hyperfocuses on what we should and shouldn't do instead of what Christ has already done. It neglects the gospel and places personal striving above the finished work of Christ.

We tell Christians that talking about sexuality deserves its own conference or sermon series, but then we don't make space for our congregants to discuss it in their daily lives. Instead of relegating the topic to youth groups or the occasional "sexy" sermon series, sexuality should become an integrated part of our Christian conversation. Instead of sending adolescents to purity conferences or handing them a copy of *Every Man's Battle* or *And the Bride Wore White*, Christians should bring these books, articles, and ideas into real-life conversations with their local church body, examining them together.

The solution is not necessarily to talk about sex more often but more honestly, and in community. As we move away from hushed tones, downcast eyes, and nervous laughter, we can view sexuality more biblically—as something God-given, common to humankind, and good. We can also be real with one another about the difficulties we face in honoring God with our sexuality. My friend Maralee said that it isn't just about having "the talk" but about creating an open, ongoing conversation with her children. This is a wonderful model both for parenting and also for the church.

We are a body. We have bodies. It is high time we walk together as embodied, sexual beings into the light of God's gospel, his truth, and his family.

TETHERED

Loneliness is real, but lust does not love you. Its only desire is to tear you apart, limb from limb. We know that when the moment of temptation passes like a ship in the night, the fog will clear and we will see Jesus again. We know that we need the church because apart from her we are just a wobbly leg or useless finger.

The pursuit of sexual purity is not about virginity or reward but about so tethering ourselves to the power of the Holy Spirit and the truth of God's Word that when the sweet music of sin enters our ears, we are able to keep steering the ship toward God's glory—because God has become a thousand times more captivating. It is about knowing that when we sin, we have an advocate; that there is forgiveness in Christ, no matter what we've done. It is about picking up the cross of Jesus each new day, and pressing into his body, the church. And it is about believing with all our hearts, that we are image bearers of a holy God, created for his glory.

DISCUSSION QUESTIONS

1. Is an open conversation about sexuality in our churches really possible? Are there practical steps we could take in our local churches to move toward this?
2. Discuss Joshua Harris's idea about being willing to reevaluate your beliefs. What are the benefits and possible dangers?

3. How can we emphasize grace in our call for Christian chastity?
4. Do you think there is a place for purity conferences in the future? Why or why not?
5. What is one thing you disagreed with in this book and why?
6. What is one thing you agree with and why?
7. What is one thing you plan to do in response to this book?

ACTIVITY

Pass index cards around the room. Have each person write down one thing they want prayer for in regard to any of the topics addressed in this book, whether it is relational loneliness, sexual sin, past abuse, or unmet longings. Have people get into pairs and share their request with their partner, taking turns praying for one another. Have everyone hang on to the card of the person they prayed for, so they can continue to pray for that person and maybe even check in on them later.

ACKNOWLEDGMENTS

So many of you took the time to talk with me about your experiences with purity culture. Whether it was over Zoom, email, or coffee in person, you let me ask the tough questions, you answered them honestly, and in so doing, gave this book its flesh and blood. I am so very grateful to you. Thank you for entrusting me with your stories. I hope I have honored them.

To my professor and advisor at The University of St. Andrews, thank you for helping me with this important research, for pushing me to be a better thinker and writer, and for always showing me such respect, despite our theological differences.

To my editor at IVP, thank you for taking a chance on me, for believing in this project, and making it a reality.

To my family and friends who spent the last two years listening to me talk on and on about this subject, reading my early chapters, and cheering me on when I grew weary: thank you for your unconditional support and your patience. You are Christ's love to me.

And to my husband, always patient, wise, and long-suffering, thank you for believing I could write this book—for never doubting it for a second—for believing I could do anything. You are my best friend, my favorite person, my home.

NOTES

FOREWORD

[1]Randall Patterson, "Students of Virginity," *New York Times*, March 30, 2008, www.nytimes.com/2008/03/30/magazine/30Chastity-t.html.

INTRODUCTION: IT'S TIME TO TALK BACK

[1]I interviewed a diverse group of people for this project, and I'm grateful to those who shared their stories and engaged me about these deeply personal subjects. Some names have been changed to protect the privacy of those interviewed. The individuals quoted and interviewed in this book do not necessarily endorse the ideas I present here, and my interaction with them does not necessarily imply an endorsement of their beliefs and ideas. But it is their experiences that give this book flesh and bones, and their perspectives that enriched my writing at every turn.

1. FROM RINGS AND PLEDGES TO CONVERSATION IN COMMUNITY

[1]Kathryn R. Klement and Brad J. Sagarin, "Nobody Wants to Date a Whore: Rape-Supportive Messages in Women-Directed Christian Dating Books," *Sexuality & Culture* 21, no. 1 (2016): 205-23.

[2]Christine Joy Gardner, *Making Chastity Sexy: The Rhetoric of Evangelical Abstinence Campaigns* (Berkeley: University of California Press, 2011), 3.

[3]Rebecca Lemke, *The Scarlet Virgins: When Sex Replaces Salvation* (Norman, OK: Anatole, 2017), 24.

[4]Krystina Rankin, Twitter, November 24, 2018, 10:55 a.m., https://twitter.com/krystinarenae/status/1066420087358406656.

[5]Claire Berger, Twitter, November 24, 2018, 10:05 a.m., https://twitter.com/ce_berger/status/1066392314245984257.

[6]Brianna Lambert, Twitter, November 24, 2018, 11:16 a.m., https://twitter.com/look_to_harvest/status/1066410357181292544.

[7]Kelly Wolfe, Twitter, November 24, 2018, 10:11 a.m., https://twitter.com/kellykwolfe/status/1066393822098264069.

[8]Kaitlin Ruiz, Twitter, November 24, 2018, 10:53 a.m., https://twitter.com/Kaitlin_M_Ruiz/status/1066404435461636096.

[9]Lucy Crabtree, Twitter, November 24, 2018, 10:27 a.m., https://twitter.com/tolivequietly/status/1066397900375302144.

[10]Nadia Bolz-Weber, Twitter, November 26, 2018, 6:53 a.m., https://twitter.com/Sarcasticluther/status/1067068789915668480.

[11]Joshua Harris, "A Statement on I Kissed Dating Goodbye," accessed December 7, 2018, https://joshharris.com/statement/.

[12]Daniel Avery, "Purity Expert Josh Harris Announces 'I Am Not a Christian,' Apologizes to LGBT Community," *Newsweek*, July 29, 2019, www.newsweek.com/josh-harris-not-christian-dating-1451553.

[13]This film is available for free online at www.youtube.com/watch?v=ybYTkkQJw_M and is also available for purchase on DVD at http://explorationfilms.com/survived/index2.php.

2. THE IDOLIZATION OF VIRGINITY

[1]Amy Deneson, "True Love Waits? The Story of My Purity Ring and Feeling Like I Didn't Have a Choice," *The Guardian*, February 18, 2017, www.theguardian.com/lifeandstyle/2017/feb/18/purity-ring-virginity-abstinence-sexual-education.

[2]Rebecca Lemke, *The Scarlet Virgins: When Sex Replaces Salvation* (Norman, OK: Anatole, 2017), 26.

[3]Sara Moslener, *Virgin Nation: Sexual Purity and American Adolescence* (New York: Oxford University Press, 2015), 105.

[4]Christine Joy Gardner, *Making Chastity Sexy: The Rhetoric of Evangelical Abstinence Campaigns* (Berkeley: University of California Press, 2011), 127.

[5]Debra Hirsch, *Redeeming Sex: Naked Conversations About Sexuality and Spirituality* (Downers Grove, IL: InterVarsity Press, 2015), 120.

[6]Daniel Darling, *The Dignity Revolution: Reclaiming God's Rich Vision for Humanity* (Epsom, UK: Good Book, 2018), 24.

[7]Linda Kay Klein, *Pure: Inside the Evangelical Movement That Shamed a Generation of Young Women and How I Broke Free* (New York: Atria Books, 2018), 311.

[8]Moslener, *Virgin Nation*, 112, 148.

[9]Jessie Hellmann, "Abstinence-Only Education Making a Comeback Under Trump," *The Hill*, March 08, 2018, https://thehill.com/policy/healthcare/377304-abstinence-only-education-making-a-comeback-under-trump.

[10]Gardner, *Making Chastity Sexy*, 6-10.

[11]Moslener, *Virgin Nation*, 6, 93, 159.

[12]Gardner, *Making Chastity Sexy*, 15.

[13]"Chapter Forty-Seven," *Jane the Virgin*, directed by Eva Longoria, aired October 31, 2016, on the CW.

[14]Klein, *Pure*, 137.

[15]Deneson, "True Love Waits?"

[16]Dan B. Allender and Tremper Longman III, *God Loves Sex: An Honest Conversation About Sexual Desire and Holiness* (Grand Rapids, MI: Baker Books, 2014), 44.

[17]Gardner, *Making Chastity Sexy*, 126.

[18]Lauren F. Winner, *Real Sex: The Naked Truth About Chastity* (Grand Rapids, MI: Brazos, 2005), 154.

3. FEMALE RESPONSIBILITIES

[1]This idea is called "gender essentialism"; see Sara Moslener, *Virgin Nation: Sexual Purity and American Adolescence* (New York: Oxford University Press, 2015), 163.

[2]Moslener, *Virgin Nation*, 98-99.

[3]Moslener, *Virgin Nation*, 17.

[4]Christine Joy Gardner, *Making Chastity Sexy: The Rhetoric of Evangelical Abstinence Campaigns* (Berkeley: University of California Press, 2011), 10, 79.

[5]Joshua Harris, *I Kissed Dating Goodbye* (Colorado Springs: Multnomah, 1997, 2003), 98.

[6]John Eldredge, *Wild at Heart: Discovering the Secret of a Man's Soul* (Nashville: Thomas Nelson, 2001), 91; Stephen Arterburn and Fred Stoeker, *Every Man's Battle: Winning the War on Sexual Temptation One Victory at a Time* (Colorado Springs: WaterBrook, 2000), 105.

[7]Nancy R. Pearcey, *Love Thy Body: Answering Hard Questions About Life and Sexuality* (Grand Rapids, MI: Baker Books, 2018), 146.

[8]Rebecca St. James, *Wait for Me: Rediscovering the Power of Purity in Romance* (Nashville: Thomas Nelson, 2002), 5.

[9]"Wait for Me," lyrics by Rebecca St. James, *Wait for Me: The Best from Rebecca St. James* (ForeFront, 2003).

[10]John and Stasi Eldredge, *Captivating: Unveiling the Mystery of a Woman's Soul* (Nashville: Thomas Nelson, 2011), xi.

[11]Dannah Gresh, *And the Bride Wore White: Seven Secrets to Sexual Purity* (Chicago: Moody Publishers, 2012); Stephen Arterburn and Shannon Ethridge, *Every Young Woman's Battle: Guarding Your Mind, Heart, and Body in a Sex-Saturated World* (Colorado Springs: WaterBrook, 2009), 7-15.

[12]Sarah Mally, *Before You Meet Prince Charming* (Cedar Rapids, IA: Tomorrow's Forefathers, 2006), 39.

[13]Shaunti Feldhahn and Lisa A. Rice, *For Young Women Only: What You Need to Know About How Guys Think* (Atlanta: Multnomah, 2006), 12-14.

[14]Mally, *Prince Charming*, 158, 159, 171.

[15]Elisabeth Elliot, *Let Me Be a Woman: Notes to My Daughter on the Meaning of Womanhood* (Carol Stream, IL: Tyndale House, 1999), 24, 31.

[16]Eldredge and Eldredge, *Captivating*, 145.

[17]Eldredge and Eldredge, *Captivating*, 114, 124, 127.

[18]Arterburn and Ethridge, *Every Young Woman's Battle*, 54.

[19]Arterburn and Ethridge, *Every Young Woman's Battle*, 14.

[20]Arterburn and Ethridge, *Every Young Woman's Battle*, 193.

[21]St. James, *Wait for Me*, 17, 20.

[22]Arterburn and Ethridge, *Every Young Woman's Battle*, 9.

[23]Gresh, *Bride Wore White*, 56.

[24]Dannah Gresh and Julianna Slattery, *Pulling Back the Shades: Erotica, Intimacy, and the Longings of a Woman's Heart* (Chicago: Moody Publishers, 2014), 9.

[25]Rebecca Lemke, *The Scarlet Virgins: When Sex Replaces Salvation* (Norman, OK: Anatole, 2017), 78.

[26]Mally, *Prince Charming*, 45.

[27]Arterburn and Ethridge, *Every Young Woman's Battle*, 137.

[28]Eric Ludy and Leslie Ludy, *Romance God's Way* (Longmont, CO: Makarios, 1997), 47.

[29]Ludy and Ludy, *Romance*, 118.

[30]Mally, *Prince Charming*, 184-85.

[31]Mally, *Prince Charming*, 52.

[32]Gresh, *Bride Wore White*, 98.

[33]Gresh, *Bride Wore White*, 98.

[34]Mally, *Prince Charming*, 33.

[35]Gresh, *Bride Wore White*, 90; Mally, *Prince Charming*, 63.

[36]Arterburn and Ethridge, *Every Young Woman's Battle*, 35-39; Gresh, *Bride Wore White*, 86.

[37]Arterburn and Ethridge, *Every Young Woman's Battle*, 2, 75.

[38]Gresh, *Bride Wore White*, 85-86.

[39]Feldhahn and Rice, *Young Women Only*, 147.

[40]Gresh, *Bride Wore White*, 55.

[41]Mally, *Prince Charming*, 194.

[42]St. James, *Wait for Me*, 53, 129.

[43]Eldredge and Eldredge, *Captivating*, 234.

[44]Arterburn and Ethridge, *Every Young Woman's Battle*, 164.

[45]Gresh, *Bride Wore White*, 23.

[46]St. James, *Wait for Me*, 119-20.

[47]Gresh, *Bride Wore White*, 163.

[48]Arterburn and Ethridge, *Every Young Woman's Battle*, 71-74.

[49]Eldredge and Eldredge, *Captivating*, 79.

[50]Arterburn and Ethridge, *Every Young Woman's Battle*, 71-74.

[51]Harris, *Kissed Dating Goodbye*, 99.

[52]Elliot, *Let Me Be a Woman*, 158.

[53]St. James, *Wait for Me*, 31.

[54]Gardner, *Making Chastity Sexy*, 76.

[55]Gardner, *Making Chastity Sexy*, 76, 134.

[56]Gardner, *Making Chastity Sexy*, 76.

[57]Harris, *Kissed Dating Goodbye*, 99.

[58]Gresh, *Bride Wore White*, 84.

[59]Feldhahn and Rice, *Young Women Only*, 98.

[60]Arterburn and Ethridge, *Every Young Woman's Battle*, 98.

[61]Lemke, *Scarlet Virgins*, 57.

[62]Linda Kay Klein, *Pure: Inside the Evangelical Movement That Shamed a Generation of Young Women and How I Broke Free* (New York: Atria Books, 2018), 3-4.

[63]Jasmine Holmes, "Black Womanhood and the War Within," *Fathom*, April 12, 2018, www.fathommag.com/stories/woman-enough-4.

[64]Alia Joy, *Glorious Weakness: Discovering God in All We Lack* (Grand Rapids, MI: Baker Books, 2019), 76.

[65]Joy, *Glorious Weakness*, 85.

[66]Eldredge and Eldredge, *Captivating*, 11, 17.

[67]Gardner, *Making Chastity Sexy*, 72.

[68]Gresh, *Bride Wore White*, 63.

[69]Elliot, *Let Me Be a Woman*, 68.

[70]Mally, *Prince Charming*, 24.

[71]Gresh, *Bride Wore White*, 86.

[72]Elliot, *Let Me Be a Woman*, 76.
[73]Mally, *Prince Charming*, 63.
[74]Eldredge and Eldredge, *Captivating*, 39, 141.
[75]Feldhahn and Rice, *Young Women Only*, 37.
[76]Feldhahn and Rice, *Young Women Only*, 27, 28, 56-58.
[77]Elliot, *Let Me Be a Woman*, 89.
[78]Eldredge and Eldredge, *Captivating*, 40.
[79]Eldredge and Eldredge, *Captivating*, 141, 151, 219.
[80]Feldhahn and Rice, *Young Women Only*, 119, 123, 126.
[81]Feldhahn and Rice, *Young Women Only*, 130-31.
[82]Arterburn and Stoeker, *Every Man's Battle*, 78, 148-49.
[83]Arterburn and Stoeker, *Every Man's Battle*, 79, 120.
[84]Eldredge and Eldredge, *Captivating*, 231-36.
[85]Mally, *Prince Charming*, 61.
[86]Mally, *Prince Charming*, 54.
[87]Arterburn and Ethridge, *Every Young Woman's Battle*, 33, 89, 190, 193.
[88]Feldhahn and Rice, *Young Women Only*, 25, 33.
[89]Justin S. Holcomb and Lindsey Holcomb, *Rid of My Disgrace: Hope and Healing for Victims of Sexual Assault* (Wheaton, IL: Crossway, 2011), 85.
[90]Church and Society Council, "Living a Theology That Counters Violence Against Women," revised version (Edinburgh: Church of Scotland, 2014), www.churchofscotland.org.uk/__data/assets/pdf_file/0017/20096/Living-a-theology.pdf.
[91]Holcomb and Holcomb, *Rid of My Disgrace*, 85-86.

4. MALE PURITY AND THE RHETORIC OF LUST

[1]John Eldredge, *Wild at Heart: Discovering the Secret of a Man's Soul* (Nashville: Thomas Nelson, 2001), 7-8.
[2]Eldredge, *Wild at Heart*, 12, 24, 27, 29, 84, 192.
[3]"NEWS: Radical, Every Man's Battle, Every Young Man's Battle, and Every Young Woman's Battle Receive ECPA Sales Awards," WaterBrook & Multnomah, August 18, 2016, https://waterbrookmultnomah.com/news-radical-every-man%E2%80%99s-battle-every-young-man%E2%80%99s-battle-and-every-young-woman%E2%80%99s-battle-receive-ecpa-sales-awards/.
[4]Joshua Harris, *I Kissed Dating Goodbye* (Colorado Springs: Multnomah, 1997, 2003), 22.
[5]Christine Joy Gardner, *Making Chastity Sexy: The Rhetoric of Evangelical Abstinence Campaigns* (Berkeley: University of California Press, 2011), 69.

[6]Eldredge, *Wild at Heart*, 16, 141.

[7]Rebecca St. James, *Wait for Me: Rediscovering the Power of Purity in Romance* (Nashville: Thomas Nelson, 2002), 2.

[8]Eldredge, *Wild at Heart*, 9.

[9]Eldredge, *Wild at Heart*, 43.

[10]Eldredge, *Wild at Heart*, 44, 187.

[11]Eldredge, *Wild at Heart*, 101, 147; Stephen Arterburn and Fred Stoeker, *Every Man's Battle: Winning the War on Sexual Temptation One Victory at a Time* (Colorado Springs: WaterBrook, 2000), 70.

[12]Arterburn and Stoeker, *Every Man's Battle*, 62, 70.

[13]Arterburn and Stoeker, *Every Man's Battle*, 74.

[14]Harris, *Kissed Dating Goodbye*, 91.

[15]Arterburn and Stoeker, *Every Man's Battle*, 13, 92, 105.

[16]Eldredge, *Wild at Heart*, 192.

[17]Eldredge, *Wild at Heart*, 18, 36, 192.

[18]Eldredge, *Wild at Heart*, 182.

[19]Eldredge, *Wild at Heart*, 17, 80, 82, 192, 185.

[20]Eldredge, *Wild at Heart*, 37.

[21]Eldredge, *Wild at Heart*, 191-92.

[22]Arterburn and Stoeker, *Every Man's Battle*, 10, 11.

[23]Arterburn and Stoeker, *Every Man's Battle*, 125.

[24]Arterburn and Stoeker, *Every Man's Battle*, 130, 156, 162.

[25]Gardner, *Making Chastity Sexy*, 81.

[26]Harris, *Kissed Dating Goodbye*, 15, 20, 65, 169.

[27]Katelyn Beaty, "A Christian Case Against the Pence Rule," *New York Times*, November 15, 2017, www.nytimes.com/2017/11/15/opinion/pence-rule-christian-graham.html.

[28]Beaty, "Christian Case."

[29]Debra Hirsch, *Redeeming Sex: Naked Conversations About Sexuality and Spirituality* (Downers Grove, IL: InterVarsity Press, 2015), 38.

[30]"Kimmy Meets an Old Friend!," *The Unbreakable Kimmy Schmidt*, directed by Jude Weng, aired May 30, 2018, on Netflix.

[31]Linda Kay Klein, *Pure: Inside the Evangelical Movement That Shamed a Generation of Young Women and How I Broke Free* (New York: Atria Books, 2018), 235.

[32]Daniel Darling, *The Dignity Revolution: Reclaiming God's Rich Vision for Humanity* (Epsom, UK: Good Book, 2018), 15.

[33]Darling, *Dignity Revolution*, 15.

5. FIRST COMES LOVE, THEN COMES MARRIAGE

[1]Sam Allberry, *7 Myths About Singleness* (Wheaton, IL: Crossway, 2019), 18.

[2]Dannah Gresh, *And the Bride Wore White: Seven Secrets to Sexual Purity* (Chicago: Moody Publishers, 2012), 139.

[3]Maura A. Ryan, "Faith and Infertility," in *On Moral Medicine: Theological Perspectives on Medical Ethics*, ed. M. Therese Lysaught et al., 3rd ed. (Grand Rapids, MI: Eerdmans, 2012), 867.

[4]Ryan, "Faith and Infertility," 867.

[5]Stanley Hauerwas, "Salvation and Health: Why Medicine Needs the Church," in Lysaught et al., *Moral Medicine*, 43.

[6]Hauerwas, "Salvation and Health," 43.

[7]Ryan, "Faith and Infertility," 868.

[8]Coralie Cowan, "How John MacArthur Made Me Cry," *Life More Abundant* (blog), September 22, 2006, https://lifemoreabundant.wordpress.com/2006/09/22/how-john-macarthur-made-me-cry/.

[9]Jackie Hill Perry, *Gay Girl, Good God: The Story of Who I Was and Who God Has Always Been* (Nashville: Good News, 2018), 11.

[10]Perry, *Gay Girl*, 83.

[11]Perry, *Gay Girl*, 87.

[12]Christine Joy Gardner, *Making Chastity Sexy: The Rhetoric of Evangelical Abstinence Campaigns* (Berkeley: University of California Press, 2011), 138.

[13]Nancy R. Pearcey, *Love Thy Body: Answering Hard Questions About Life and Sexuality* (Grand Rapids, MI: Baker Books, 2018), 148.

[14]Wesley Hill, "General Session 3," Revoice conference, YouTube video, July 30, 2018, www.youtube.com/watch?v=xvEUnnA8nFo.

[15]Pearcey, *Love Thy Body*, 11.

[16]Nadia Bolz-Weber, *Shameless: A Sexual Reformation* (New York: Convergent Books, 2019), 71.

[17]Molly Jasinski, "What Ifs and White Dresses," *Rise* (blog), March 26, 2019, www.nowsherises.org/rise-blog/what-ifs-and-white-dresses.

[18]Lauren F. Winner, *Real Sex: The Naked Truth About Chastity* (Grand Rapids, MI: Brazos, 2005), 128-29.

[19]Karen Swallow Prior, "Called to Childlessness: The Surprising Ways of God," Ethics and Religious Liberty Commission of the Southern Baptist Convention, March 6, 2017, https://erlc.com/resource-library/articles/called-to-childlessness-the-surprising-ways-of-god.

[20]Perry, *Gay Girl*, 190.

6. PROBLEMS WITH THE PROMISE OF SEX

[1]Christine Joy Gardner, *Making Chastity Sexy: The Rhetoric of Evangelical Abstinence Campaigns* (Berkeley: University of California Press, 2011), i, ix, 8-11.

[2]Sara Moslener, *Virgin Nation: Sexual Purity and American Adolescence* (New York: Oxford University Press, 2015), 26.

[3]Gardner, *Making Chastity Sexy*, i, 53, 104, 188.

[4]Rob Haskell, "Justin and Hailey Bieber Open Up About Their Passionate, Not-Always-Easy but Absolutely All-In Romance," *Vogue*, February 7, 2019, www.vogue.com/article/justin-bieber-hailey-bieber-cover-interview.

[5]Dannah Gresh, *And the Bride Wore White: Seven Secrets to Sexual Purity* (Chicago: Moody Publishers, 2012), 14, 127; Rebecca St. James, *Wait for Me: Rediscovering the Power of Purity in Romance* (Nashville: Thomas Nelson, 2002), 8.

[6]Sarah Mally, *Before You Meet Prince Charming* (Cedar Rapids, IA: Tomorrow's Forefathers, 2006), 193.

[7]Joshua Harris, *I Kissed Dating Goodbye* (Colorado Springs: Multnomah, 1997, 2003), 83, 202.

[8]Stephen Arterburn and Fred Stoeker, *Every Man's Battle: Winning the War on Sexual Temptation One Victory at a Time* (Colorado Springs: WaterBrook, 2000), 17.

[9]Lauren F. Winner, *Real Sex: The Naked Truth About Chastity* (Grand Rapids, MI: Brazos, 2005), 86-89.

[10]Sinclair B. Ferguson, *The Whole Christ: Legalism, Antinomianism, and Gospel Assurance—Why the Marrow Controversy Still Matters* (Wheaton, IL: Crossway, 2016), 49.

[11]Joy Pedrow Skarka, "Having Painful Sex," *Fathom*, February 12, 2018, www.fathommag.com/stories/having-painful-sex.

[12]Caroline Judelson, "Woman Says Agonizing Condition Has Left Her Unable to Have Sex," Fox News, June 26, 2018, www.foxnews.com/health/woman-says-agonizing-condition-has-left-her-unable-to-have-sex.

[13]Winner, *Real Sex*, 119.

[14]Niraj Chokshi, "What Is an Incel? A Term Used by the Toronto Van Attack Suspect, Explained," *New York Times*, April 24, 2018, www.nytimes.com/2018/04/24/world/canada/incel-reddit-meaning-rebellion.html.

[15]Joy Beth Smith, *Party of One: Truth, Longing, and the Subtle Art of Singleness* (Nashville: Thomas Nelson, 2018), 6.

[16]Smith, *Party of One*, 13.

[17]Rebecca Lemke, *The Scarlet Virgins: When Sex Replaces Salvation* (Norman, OK: Anatole, 2017), 70-72.

7. WHAT THE SEXUALLY ABUSED HEAR

[1]Justin S. Holcomb and Lindsey Holcomb, *Rid of My Disgrace: Hope and Healing for Victims of Sexual Assault* (Wheaton, IL: Crossway, 2011), 33.

[2]Holcomb and Holcomb, *Rid of My Disgrace*, 215.

[3]Sara Moslener, *Virgin Nation: Sexual Purity and American Adolescence* (New York: Oxford University Press, 2015), 122.

[4]Christine Joy Gardner, *Making Chastity Sexy: The Rhetoric of Evangelical Abstinence Campaigns* (Berkeley: University of California Press, 2011), 34.

[5]Gardner, *Making Chastity Sexy*, 50.

[6]Sarah Mally, *Before You Meet Prince Charming* (Cedar Rapids, IA: Tomorrow's Forefathers, 2006), 193.

[7]Abby Ohlheiser, "The Montana Judge Who Blamed a 14-Year-Old for Her Own Rape Will Be Censured," *The Atlantic*, June 4, 2014, www.theatlantic.com/politics/archive/2014/06/the-montana-judge-who-blamed-a-14-year-old-for-her-own-rape-will-be-censured/372185/.

[8]Eliza Gray, "The Sexual Assault Crisis on American Campuses," *Time*, May 15, 2014, 20-27.

[9]Alexandra Brodsky, "Blame Rape's Enablers, Not the Victims," *New York Times*, October 23, 2013, www.nytimes.com/roomfordebate/2013/10/23/young-women-drinking-and-rape/blame-rapes-enablers-not-the-victims.

[10]Abby Perry, "Prophetic Survivors: Ruthy Nordgren," *Fathom*, January 28, 2019, www.fathommag.com/stories/prophetic-survivors-ruthy-nordgren; Matthew Myers, "Investigation Uncovers Hundreds of Sexual Abuse Allegations in Baptist Churches; Former Local Bible Teacher Cited," 9 & 10 News, December 11, 2018, www.9and10news.com/2018/12/11/investigation-uncovers-hundreds-of-sexual-abuse-allegations-in-baptist-churches-former-local-bible-teacher-cited/.

[11]Abby Perry, "Prophetic Survivors: Jules Woodson," *Fathom Magazine*, September 24, 2018, www.fathommag.com/stories/prophetic-survivors-jules-woodson.

[12]Perry, "Woodson."

[13]Danielle Young, "Don't Let the Smile Fool You. I'm Cringing on the Inside," *The Root*, November 6, 2017, www.theroot.com/don-t-let-the-smile-fool-you-i-m-cringing-on-the-insid-1819987586.

[14]Gardner, *Making Chastity Sexy*, 86.

[15]Holcomb and Holcomb, *Rid of My Disgrace*, 72.

[16]Jonathan Trotter, "The Lies Modesty Culture Teaches Men," *Relevant*, April 11, 2019, https://relevantmagazine.com/god/worldview/lies-modesty-culture-teaches-men.

[17]Parts of this section previously appeared in Rachel Joy Welcher, "3 Lies About Sexual Assault the Church Must Stop Perpetuating," *Relevant*, November 15, 2017, https://relevantmagazine.com/current/image-god-age-sexual-assault/.

[18]Jessica Valenti, *The Purity Myth: How America's Obsession with Virginity Is Hurting Young Women* (Berkeley, CA: Seal, 2010), 149-51. Ironically, Matt Lauer himself has more recently been accused of misusing his positional power to commit sexual assault against multiple women; see Ramin Setoodeh and Elizabeth Wagmeister, "Matt Lauer Accused of Sexual Harassment by Multiple Women," *Variety*, December 12, 2017, http://variety.com/2017/biz/news/matt-lauer-accused-sexual-harassment-multiple-women-1202625959/.

[19]Valenti, *Purity Myth*, 151.

[20]Stephen Arterburn and Shannon Ethridge, *Every Young Woman's Battle: Guarding Your Mind, Heart, and Body in a Sex-Saturated World* (Colorado Springs: Waterbrook, 2009), 98.

[21]Kathryn R. Klement and Brad J. Sagarin, "Nobody Wants to Date a Whore: Rape-Supportive Messages in Women-Directed Christian Dating Books," *Sexuality & Culture* 21, no. 1 (2016): 219.

[22]Morah Conant, Twitter, May 30, 2018, 12:35 p.m., https://twitter.com/owls2fly/status/1001910038737379328.

[23]Harry Dreyfuss, "Actor Harry Dreyfuss: When I Was 18, Kevin Spacey Groped Me," *Buzzfeed News*, November 4, 2017, www.buzzfeednews.com/article/harrydreyfuss2/actor-harry-dreyfuss-when-i-was-18-kevin-spacey-groped-me.

[24]Parts of this section previously appeared in Rachel Joy Welcher, "3 Lies About Sexual Assault the Church Must Stop Perpetuating," *Relevant*, November 15, 2017, https://relevantmagazine.com/current/image-god-age-sexual-assault/.

[25]Holcomb and Holcomb, *Rid of My Disgrace*, 21-22, 28.

[26]Sarah Bowler, "Bathsheba: Vixen or Victim?" in *Vindicating the Vixens: Revisiting Sexualized, Vilified, and Marginalized Women of the Bible* (Grand Rapids, MI: Kregel, 2017), 99-100.

[27]Richard Bauckham, *Gospel Women: Studies of the Named Women in the Gospels* (Grand Rapids, MI: Eerdmans, 2003), 19.

[28]John Eldredge, *Wild at Heart: Discovering the Secret of a Man's Soul* (Nashville: Thomas Nelson, 2001), 190.

[29]Richard M. Davidson, "Did King David Rape Bathsheba? A Case Study in Narrative Theology," *Journal of the Adventist Theological Society* 17, no. 2 (2006): 93.

[30]Davidson, "Did King David Rape Bathsheba?," 91.

[31]Bauckham, *Gospel Women*, 24.

[32]Joshua Harris, *I Kissed Dating Goodbye* (Colorado Springs: Multnomah, 1997, 2003), 90.

[33]David Powlison, *Making All Things New: Restoring Joy to the Sexually Broken* (Wheaton, IL: Crossway, 2017), 17.

[34]Alexander I. Abasili, "Was It Rape? The David and Bathsheba Pericope Re-examined," *Vetus Testamentum* 61, no. 1 (2011): 4, 10.

[35]Bowler, "Bathsheba," 84-85.

[36]Davidson, "Did King David Rape Bathsheba?," 88-89.

[37]Bauckham, *Gospel Women*, 27.

[38]Bowler, "Bathsheba," 96.

[39]Bowler, "Bathsheba," 96.

[40]Dannah Gresh, *And the Bride Wore White: Seven Secrets to Sexual Purity* (Chicago: Moody Publishers, 2012), 37.

[41]Mally, *Prince Charming*, 195.

[42]Bowler, "Bathsheba," 81, 83; George G. Nicol, "The Alleged Rape of Bathsheba: Some Observations on Ambiguity in Biblical Narrative," *Journal for the Study of the Old Testament* 22, no. 73 (1997): 43-44; Bauckham, *Gospel Women*, 27.

[43]Bowler, "Bathsheba," 81, 82, 95; Davidson, "Did King David Rape Bathsheba?," 84.

[44]Bowler, "Bathsheba," 92.

[45]Powlison, *Making All Things New*, 35.

[46]Holcomb and Holcomb, *Rid of My Disgrace*, 109.

[47]Katelyn Beaty, "A Christian Case Against the Pence Rule," *New York Times*, November 15, 2017, www.nytimes.com/2017/11/15/opinion/pence-rule-christian-graham.html; Holcomb and Holcomb, *Rid of My Disgrace*, 29.

[48]Arterburn and Ethridge, *Every Young Woman's Battle*, 98.

[49]Bowler, "Bathsheba," 98.

[50]Caryn Tamber-Rosenau, "Biblical Bathing Beauties and the Manipulation of the Male Gaze: What Judith Can Tell Us About Bathsheba and Susanna," *Journal of Feminist Studies in Religion* 33, no. 2 (2017): 61.

[51]Tamber-Rosenau, "Bathing Beauties," 61.

[52]Jeremy Posadas, “Teaching the Cause of Rape Culture: Toxic Masculinity,” *Journal of Feminist Studies in Religion* 33, no. 1 (2017): 177.

[53]Rachael Denhollander, “Read Rachael Denhollander’s Full Victim Impact Statement About Larry Nassar,” CNN, video, January 30, 2018, www.cnn.com/2018/01/24/us/rachael-denhollander-full-statement/.

[54]Jules Woodson, “I Was Assaulted. He Was Applauded,” *New York Times*, video, March 9, 2018, www.nytimes.com/2018/03/09/opinion/jules-woodson-andy-savage-assault.html.

[55]Powlison, *Making All Things New*, 103.

8. SUBMITTING TO GOD’S SEXUAL ETHIC AS EMBODIED SOULS

[1]Joy Beth Smith, *Party of One: Truth, Longing, and the Subtle Art of Singleness* (Nashville: Thomas Nelson, 2018), 93.

[2]Smith, *Party of One*, 94.

[3]Nancy R. Pearcey, *Love Thy Body: Answering Hard Questions About Life and Sexuality* (Grand Rapids, MI: Baker Books, 2018), 139.

[4]Daniel Darling, *The Dignity Revolution: Reclaiming God’s Rich Vision for Humanity* (Epsom, UK: Good Book, 2018), 150.

[5]Linda Kay Klein, *Pure: Inside the Evangelical Movement That Shamed a Generation of Young Women and How I Broke Free* (New York: Atria Books, 2018), 34, 198.

[6]Nadia Bolz-Weber, *Shameless: A Sexual Reformation* (New York: Convergent Books, 2019), 59.

[7]Bolz-Weber, *Shameless*, 19-20.

[8]Michael Green, *2 Peter and Jude: An Introduction and Commentary*, Tyndale New Testament Commentaries (Downers Grove, IL: InterVarsity Press, 1987), 217.

[9]Sinclair B. Ferguson, *The Whole Christ: Legalism, Antinomianism, and Gospel Assurance—Why the Marrow Controversy Still Matters* (Wheaton, IL: Crossway, 2016), 157.

[10]Ferguson, *Whole Christ*, 16.

[11]Scott Sauls, “Sex, Scripture, and Modern Times,” blog, March 8, 2019, http://scottsauls.com/blog/2019/03/08/somethoughtsonsex/.

[12]Bolz-Weber, *Shameless*, 16-17.

[13]Ferguson, *Whole Christ*, 69, 81.

[14]Ferguson, *Whole Christ*, 173.

[15]Bolz-Weber, *Shameless*, 5.

[16]Tish Harrison Warren, “The Church Made Vagina Sculptures Long Before Nadia Bolz-Weber,” *Christianity Today*, February 26, 2019, www.christianity

today.com/women/2019/february/nadia-bolz-weber-church-made-vagina-sculptures.html.

[17]Warren, "Vagina Sculptures."

9. WHAT WILL WE TELL OUR CHILDREN?

[1]Jackie Hill Perry, *Gay Girl, Good God: The Story of Who I Was and Who God Has Always Been* (Nashville: Good News, 2018), 116.

[2]Abby Perry, "Prophetic Survivors: Ruthy Nordgren," *Fathom*, January 28, 2019, www.fathommag.com/stories/prophetic-survivors-ruthy-nordgren.

[3]Joy Beth Smith, *Party of One: Truth, Longing, and the Subtle Art of Singleness* (Nashville: Thomas Nelson, 2018), 88.

[4]Rebecca Lemke, *The Scarlet Virgins: When Sex Replaces Salvation* (Norman, OK: Anatole, 2017), 3.

[5]Linda Kay Klein, *Pure: Inside the Evangelical Movement That Shamed a Generation of Young Women and How I Broke Free* (New York: Atria Books, 2018), 193.

[6]Debra Hirsch, *Redeeming Sex: Naked Conversations About Sexuality and Spirituality* (Downers Grove, IL: InterVarsity Press, 2015), 40.

[7]Nancy R. Pearcey, *Love Thy Body: Answering Hard Questions About Life and Sexuality* (Grand Rapids, MI: Baker Books, 2018), 121.

[8]Hirsch, *Redeeming Sex*, 71.

[9]Hirsch, *Redeeming Sex*, 26.

[10]Aimee Byrd's book *Why Can't We Be Friends?: Avoidance Is Not Purity* (Phillipsburg, NJ: P&R, 2018) is great on this topic.

[11]Sam Allberry, "May SSA Christians Have Non-Sexual Romantic Relationships?" The Gospel Coalition, March 23, 2019, www.thegospelcoalition.org/article/non-sexual-romantic-relationships/.

[12]Lauren F. Winner, *Real Sex: The Naked Truth About Chastity* (Grand Rapids, MI: Brazos, 2005), 52.

[13]Perry, *Gay Girl*, 101.

[14]Nona Willis Aronowitz, "How to Get an Abortion If You're a Teen," *Teen Vogue*, June 6, 2019, www.teenvogue.com/story/how-to-get-an-abortion-if-youre-a-teen; Yana Tallon-Hicks, "How to Have Sex If You're Queer: What to Know About Protection, Consent, and What Queer Sex Means," *Teen Vogue*, June 4, 2019, www.teenvogue.com/story/how-to-have-queer-sex; Emily Depasse, "What to Say If Your Friend Has Herpes," *Teen Vogue*, April 16, 2019, www.teenvogue.com/story/what-to-say-if-your-friend-has-herpes; Nona Willis Aronowitz, "When Is It Safe to Send a

Partner Nude Photos?" *Teen Vogue*, May 2, 2019, www.teenvogue.com/story/when-is-it-safe-to-send-nude-photos-dtfo.

[15]Pearcey, *Love Thy Body*, 118.

[16]Pearcey, *Love Thy Body*, 127.

[17]Barna Group and Josh McDowell, *The Porn Phenomenon: The Impact of Pornography in the Digital Age* (Ventura, CA: Barna, 2016), 85.

[18]Russell Brand, "Actor Russell Brand Reveals Why He No Longer Watches Porn," video, Fight the New Drug, August 7, 2017, https://fightthenewdrug.org/russell-brand-reveals-why-he-chooses-not-to-watch-porn/.

[19]Pearcey, *Love Thy Body*, 128.

[20]Barna and McDowell, *Porn Phenomenon*, 28, 29; Roxanne Stone, "Porn 2.0: The Sexting Crisis," Barna, April 13, 2016, www.barna.com/porn-2-0-the-sexting-crisis/.

[21]Fight the New Drug, "How Clicking Porn Directly Fuels Sex Trafficking," video, accessed August 10, 2019, https://fightthenewdrug.org/media/how-porn-fuels-sex-trafficking-video/.

[22]Rachel Welcher, Twitter poll, June 19, 2019, 7:54 a.m., https://twitter.com/racheljwelcher/status/1141358710947794944.

[23]Samuel L. Perry, *Addicted to Lust: Pornography in the Lives of Conservative Protestants* (New York: Oxford University Press, 2019), 4.

[24]Perry, *Addicted*, 19.

[25]*A.I.: Artificial Intelligence*, written and directed by Steven Spielberg (Burbank, CA: Warner Brothers, 2001).

[26]Perri Klass, "Why Is Children's Masturbation Such a Secret?" *New York Times*, December 10, 2018, www.nytimes.com/2018/12/10/well/family/why-is-childrens-masturbation-such-a-secret.html.

[27]Winner, *Real Sex*, 34

[28]Eve Tushnet, "What Could Possibly Be Wrong with Christian Masturbation?" *Christianity Today*, February 24, 2016, www.christianitytoday.com/women/2016/february/what-could-possibly-be-wrong-with-christian-masturbation.html.

[29]Abby Perry, "Woven: The Threat of a Female Body," *Entropy*, May 22, 2019, https://entropymag.org/woven-the-threat-of-a-female-body/.

[30]Kim Gaines Eckert, *Things Your Mother Never Told You: A Woman's Guide to Sexuality* (Downers Grove, IL: InterVarsity Press, 2014), 11.

10. PURITY CULTURE MOVING FORWARD

[1]Jessica Van Der Wyngaard, *I Survived I Kissed Dating Goodbye,* available for free online at www.youtube.com/watch?v=ybYTkkQJw_M and also available for purchase on DVD at http://explorationfilms.com/survived/index2.php.

[2]Van Der Wyngaard, *Survived.*

[3]Daniel Darling, *The Dignity Revolution: Reclaiming God's Rich Vision for Humanity* (Epsom, UK: Good Book, 2018), 15.

[4]Lauren F. Winner, *Real Sex: The Naked Truth About Chastity* (Grand Rapids, MI: Brazos, 2005), 126.

[5]Winner, *Real Sex,* 23.

[6]Winner, *Real Sex,* 14.